THE ROYAL NAVY
SUBMARINE SERVICE

THE ROYAL NAVY
SUBMARINE SERVICE
A CENTENNIAL HISTORY

ANTONY PRESTON

CONWAY
MARITIME PRESS

This book is dedicated to all those who gave their lives in Royal Navy and Commonwealth submarines in peace and war.

© Antony Preston 2001

First published in Great Britain in 2001 by Conway Maritime Press,
a division of Chrysalis Books Plc

Conway Maritime Press,
9 Blenheim Court, Brewery Road,
London N7 9NY

www.conwaymaritime.com

A member of the Chrysalis Group plc

British Library Cataloguing in Publication Data
A record of this title is available on request from the British Library.

ISBN 0 85177 891 7

Edited by Martin Robson
Typesetting by Stephen Dent
Printed and bound in Spain by Bookprint.

Frontispiece:
D.1 *running ahead of the armoured cruiser HMS* Drake, *about 1908. The W/T aerials are slung to allow her to receive signals, but she cannot transmit.* (BAES Marine)

CONTENTS

ACKNOWLEDGEMENTS

The author wishes to thank all those who provided information for this book, notably Commander Jeff Tall OBE, RN, Director of the Royal Navy Submarine Museum (SMM) and Debbie Corner, his Keeper of Photographs, who went to such lengths to provide many of the excellent illustrations. I must also thank Mike Smith of BAE Systems Marine (BAES Marine) in Barrow in Furness, for running to earth a number of additional photographs of Barrow-built submarines, and Vic Jeffrey, the Press Officer at the Royal Australian Navy's Fleet Base West in Fremantle, WA for going to great lengths to provide photographs from his own collection and official RAN archives.

I must also recall the enormous amount of encouragement I received from my *alte kamerad* at the National Maritime Museum, the late David Lyon, who shared my enthusiasm for digging out ever more exotic submarine 'as fitted' drawings and information on sub-systems, including a diagram of a 'K' class 'heads' complete with wooden seat, cistern and chain. I must also record my gratitude to submariners past and present, who have regaled me over the years with stories, many of them too scurrilous to be included in this book, and the public relations departments of the Royal Navy and Royal Norwegian Navy, who enabled me to get some limited but invaluable 'hands on' experience of life underwater.

Apart from my friends and acquaintances too numerous to list, I must record my gratitude to the publishers, Conway Maritime Press, my editor Martin Robson for his patience and encouragement, and the designer Steve Dent, their knowledge and interest in naval history have added significantly to the quality of the book.

In compiling this book it has been impossible to account for every single event involving HM Submarines (the book would be much longer and many times more expensive), and the Author apologises to any veterans who think they or their boat may have been short-changed.

Antony Preston, London May 2001

NOTE:

All measurements are in feet and inches

All dimensions, speeds and ranges are given as surfaced, where two numbers are given the first relates to surfaced the second to submerged

ABBREVIATIONS

AA	anti-aircraft	oa	overall
AIP	air-independent propulsion	pdr	pounder(s)
bhp	brake horsepower	PWR	pressurised water-cooled reactor
c	circa	RAN	Royal Australian Navy
COMINT	communications intercept	RNZN	Royal New Zealand Navy
DNC	Director of Naval Construction	SAM	surface-to-air missile
ESM	electronic support measures	shp	shaft horsepower
ft	foot; feet	SLAM	Submarine Launched Air-defence Missile
FASM	Future Attack Submarine	SLBM	Submarine Launched Ballistic Missile
GUPPY	Greater Underwater Propulsion	SMCS	Submarine Command System
hp	horsepower	SSBN	nuclear powered strategic (ballistic) missile submarine
HTP	high test hydrogen peroxide		
ICBM	Intercontinental Ballistic Missile	SSG(N)	submarine armed with tactical missiles
in	inch(es)	SSK	hunter-killer submarine
kts	knots	SSN	nuclear powered attack submarine
NATO	North Atlantic Treaty Organisation	TLAM	Tomahawk Land Attack Missile
nm	nautical miles	TT	torpedo tube(s)

FOREWORD

FOREWORD
BY REAR ADMIRAL R P STEVENS CB

The idea of a centenary diary of the Royal Navy' Submarine Service was first put to me by Antony Preston with the enthusiastic support of Commander Jeff Tall, Director of the Submarine Museum, and I expressed my support for the idea. In the centenary year there will be many books about the service and its achievements, but none recording the significant dates in chronological order, listing the losses, successes and significant technical milestones in its first 100 years. It is marvellously comprehensive and will also function as a reference for data on all the various types of coastal, patrol, fleet, midget and nuclear submarines built for the Navy. Some were good, others not so good, but the important theme throughout is that there was a uniformly high quality of personnel over the whole century.

Today's multi role nuclear submarine is a core capability in the Royal Navy. It can be deployed anywhere in the world, strike swiftly or control the underwater environment. Technology and our new-found expertise has finally achieved that of which the submarine pioneers could only dream – to dominate the underwater battlespace. Add the daunting deterrence of the Trident Missile Submarines, and one can see that submarines are now a key tenet of the United Kingdom's Defence Policy. This book captures the chronological history of our submarines' rise to prominence.

Rear Admiral R P Stevens CB

7

MAPS

Showing the main theatres of operations
mentioned in this book:

1. The Atlantic Ocean

2. The Mediterranean

3. The North Sea and Baltic

4. The Far East

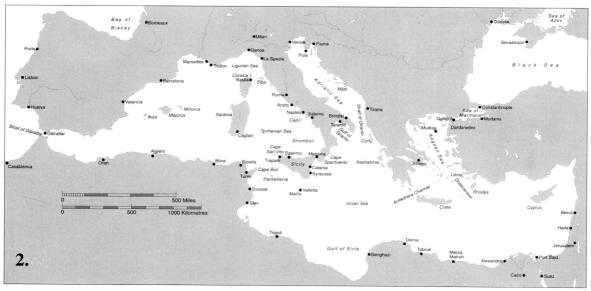

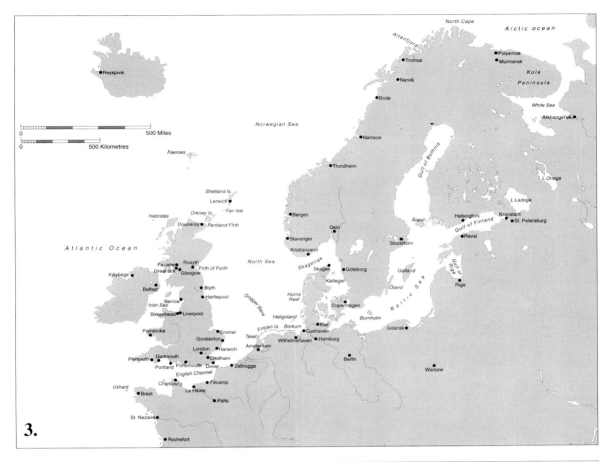

3.

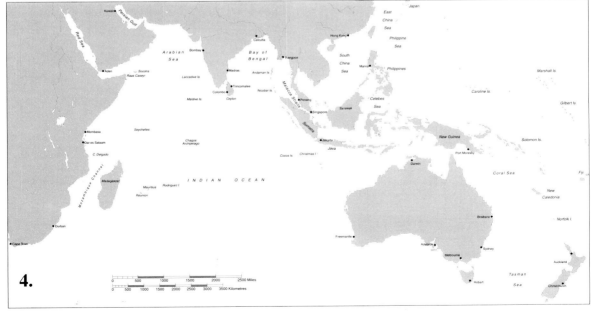

4.

INTRODUCTION

T HE GENESIS OF THIS BOOK was a meeting with Cdr Jeff Tall OBE, RN, Director of the Royal Navy Submarine Museum at Gosport in 2000, and an extremely informative Submarine Conference held at Lancaster University in the autumn of the same year.

As one who did not serve in the Royal Navy, let alone in submarines, I am often asked why I find submarines so absorbing. The answer, I suppose, is their combination of mystery (to the layman, at least), military potential and high technology. Submariners would cringe at the thought of being described as a 'special breed', but it does take a special kind of outlook to spend one's working life in artificial daylight several hundred metres under the surface of the sea. Having spent brief periods in both diesel-electric submarines and nuclear boats, I can testify to the fact that even a 4000-ton nuclear submarine is short of space. When asked if I minded the claustrophobia, I replied that one spends too much time dodging head-height or knee-height valves and other knobbly excrescence capable of crippling the unwary. The fact that no Royal Navy submarine has been lost for over 40 years is a testimony to the professionalism of submariners and the soundness of the design and construction of modern boats. For earlier generations of submariners it was a much more dangerous profession, even in peacetime, and the two world wars took a grim toll of what was always a relatively small and close-knit 'family'.

On a more serious level, the history of submarines goes back much further than most people realise. Inventors dreamed of travelling underwater for centuries, and usually their conceptions had a warlike purpose, to break blockades or to penetrate enemy harbours undetected and sink ships. Periodic attempts have been made to produce submarines for peaceful use, but with very little success, and the investment has always come from military budgets.

Ten years before the Spanish Armada was defeated, an Englishman, William Bourne, described a submersible boat in his book *Inventions and Devices*. There is no evidence that Bourne's boat was ever built, but his description leaves us in no doubt that he had grasped the essential concepts of a workable craft. A simple wooden boat-shaped hull was to be decked over and sealed to make it watertight, and leather bags were built into the bilges to act as ballast tanks by admitting water through holes in the side. As the bags filled with water the positive buoyancy would be destroyed and the craft would sink. To come back to the surface the operator would turn two screw presses to squeeze the water out of the bags.

Bourne had mastered a concept that would elude many later submarine inventors: he provided a simple mechanical means of varying the boat's total displacement. He also provided a hollow mast to replace stale air, but failed to indicate how the boat was to be propelled, and made no mention of any means of attacking a hostile ship, nor even a suggestion for peaceful use. Even with the air mast, an oarsman would soon become exhausted, and there was no other source of energy.

England was an expanding maritime power in the late sixteenth and early seventeenth centuries, and was therefore likely to attract inventors, honest or otherwise. Thus the Dutch physician Cornelius van Drebbel made his way to England, and in 1624 built two submersible boats, encased with greased leather to make them watertight. Both relied on oars to force them down, but it seems that it was more of a parlour trick than a serious step in the evolution of the submarine. There is no evidence that either boat submerged, and they could only run awash. Great exertions were needed to maintain trim. However, van Drebbel was a shrewd publicist, and is said to have persuaded King James I to travel in one of his boats, quite an achievement in the light the monarch's well-known reluctance to risk his neck. Contemporary reports claim that the boat submerged to a

The Reverend George Garrett posing on the conning tower of his Resurgam, *with two of the contractor's staff, cradling his baby son.* (SMM)

depth of 12-15ft (4-5 metres) and was rowed for *several hours*. This was physically impossible, and can be dismissed as over-enthusiastic sales promotion - an affliction that would infect many later submarine inventors.

In 1653 a Monsieur de Son took the first known step towards creating a submarine intended for warlike operations. At Rotterdam he built a boat which he claimed 'Doeth undertake in one day to destroy an hundred ships', would have the speed of a bird and would be immune to fire, storm and bullets, 'unless it please God'. The boat was a big catamaran with a clockwork engine driving a paddle wheel between the two hulls. Sadly de Son's enthusiasm had run away with him, and the clockwork engine proved too weak to move his boat, which was 72ft (24 metres) long, bigger than the Royal Navy's *Holland No.1* 250 years later. His wooden monster was large enough to provide air for two or three crew members, but the lack of an effective propulsion system doomed it to oblivion.

The Russians have habitually claimed to have invented everything before anybody else, and this is often true, so we must not be surprised to hear that Czar Peter the Great ordered a submarine at the beginning of the eighteenth century. It was actually completed in 1729, in the reign of Peter II, but was no more successful than its predecessors, and nothing more was heard of it.

One of the problems of tracing the history of early submarines is the lack of details of construction, as opposed to fanciful interpretations by later artists. In 1747, however, the *Gentlemen's Magazine* published the first drawing of a submarine, the brainchild of an inventor called Symons. It appears to draw on the ideas of both Bourne and van Drebbel, with oars for propulsion and leather bags for ballast tanks.

Around 1773 a ship's carpenter called Day experimented with a 'diving machine', and converted a small sloop by building an air-chamber amidships. Day's contribution was the concept of detachable ballast, in the form of boulders hung from external ring-bolts. The inventor achieved one successful dive in Plymouth Sound, but on 20 June 1774 disaster struck; the pressure at 22 fathoms (132ft or 43 metres) almost certainly crushed the wooden shell. The First Lord of the Admiralty, Lord Sandwich, was visiting Plymouth at the time, and authorised the use of Navy ships to assist in rescue attempts - the first recorded submarine salvage attempt.

Almost coinciding with Day's tragic attempt to defy the laws of physics, across the Atlantic a young Yale graduate was applying his mind to the problem. David Bushnell was already interested in submarines, but the War of Independence gave him the incentive to create a weapon which could break the British blockade. Bushnell left a detailed desription of his *Turtle* in a letter written in 1787 to Thomas Jefferson, then United States Minister Plenipotentiary in Paris;

'The external shape of the sub-marine vessel bore some resemblance to two upper tortoise shells of equal size, joined together; the place of entrance into the vessel being represented by the opening made by the swell of the shells, at the head of the animal. The inside was capable of containing the operator, and air sufficient to support him for 30 minutes without receiving fresh air. At the bottom opposite the entrance was fixed a quantity of lead for ballast. At one edge which was directly before the operator who sat upright, was an oar for rowing forward or backward. At the other edge was a rudder for steering. An aperture at the bottom, with its valve, was designed to admit water for the purpose of descending; and two brass forcing pumps served to eject the water within, when necessary for ascending. At the top there was likewise an oar for ascending or descending, or continuing at any particular depth. A water gauge or barometer determined the depth of descent, a compass directed the course, and a ventilator within supplied the vessel with fresh air when on the surface.

The entrance into the vessel was elliptical, and so small as barely to admit a person. This entrance was surrounded with a broad elliptical band, the lower edge of which was let into the wood of which the body of the vessel was made, in such a manner as to give its utmost support to the body of the vessel against the pressure of the water. Above the upper edge of this iron band there was a brass crown or cover, resembling a hat with its crown an brim, which shut watertight upon the iron band; the crown was hung to the iron band with hinges so as to turn over sideways when opened...

In the forepart of the brim of the crown was a socket, and an iron tube passing through the socket; the tube stood upright and could slide up and down, in the socket, about six inches. At the top of the tube was a wood-screw fixed by means of a rod which passed through the tube and screwed the wood-screw fast upon the top of the tube…

Behind the sub-marine vessel was a place above the rudder for carrying a large powder charge; this was made of two pieces of oak timber, large enough when hollowed out to contain one hundred and fifty pounds of powder...'

If we knew nothing about Bushnell, his detailed description of his one-man submarine would stamp him as a skilled and far-sighted engineer.

The *Turtle* embodied features not seen for another century: a depth-gauge, a time-fuzed detachable explosive charge, and even a primitive snort mast. Trials were carried out with ballast, before Bushnell's brother attempted a manned tethered dive, and separate trials were carried out on the explosive charge and the time-fuze.

So far so good, but Bushnell now encountered a serious snag; his brother fell ill, and we can guess that prolonged breathing of his own air was the cause. Bushnell himself was ill, and so the Army was asked to provide three 'volunteers' for the first operational submarine attack in history. Sergeant Ezra Lee drew the short straw, and on the night of 6 September 1776 he climbed into the tiny craft and was towed down the Hudson River to attack Lord Howe's fleet lying off Governor's Island. The experience must have been nightmarish, for Lee found that the current swept him past the British fleet, and he had to spend two hours working slowly back upstream. Eventually he reached Howe's flagship, the 64-gun ship HMS *Eagle*, but when he tried to penetrate her keel with the wood-screw he was defeated. For nearly 200 years it was believed that he had encountered copper sheathing on the underside of the *Eagle*, but Bushnell was sceptical, and he has been proved right. The Admiralty Progress Books show that HMS *Eagle* received no copper sheathing until she returned to England after the war.

Some have suggested that Bushnell's *Turtle* was no more than a colossal hoax, intended to panic the British into lifting their blockade, in which case, why did he take the trouble to give Jefferson such a detailed explanation? A quarter of a century ago the staff of the Smithsonian Institution in Washington DC built a full-scale model of the *Turtle* to test its feasibility, and found that all features were reproducible. Its main weakness was its complexity; the operator simply had too many tasks to carry out, and he would soon become exhausted. Modern diving knowledge suggests that Lee was suffering temporary depression from breathing carbon dioxide, and physical exhaustion. To him the *Eagle* would seem gigantic, and in all probability became discouraged when his first attempt failed.

The *Turtle* is claimed to have made another two attacks before being lost when the frigate that was carrying her was wrecked. She was not only the first submarine to attack an enemy ship, but also the first to escape. A copy, or at least a very similar craft, is said to have been used in the War of 1812. In July 1813 the 74-gun ship HMS *Ramillies*

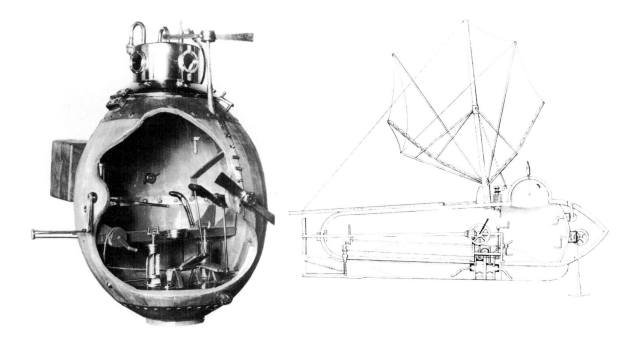

reported that she had been attacked by a 'diving boat', which succeeded in penetrating her copper sheathing, but failed to attach a charge.

Another American took the submarine a step further, although he was an ardent pacifist who thought that submarines could destroy navies and thereby rid the world of armaments. Robert Fulton regarded the French Revolution as a great force for freedom, and emigrated to France to offer his ideas in the Service of Mankind. On 13 December 1797 he wrote to the Directory, the committee that ruled France, offering them a 'mechanical engine' for the annihilation of the Royal Navy, which, through the use of close blockade, was strangling French external trade.

For a committed pacifist, Fulton was not naïve about money. He offered to build his submarine at his own expense, and to be paid 4000 francs per gun for every British ship armed with 40 guns or more. There was only one drawback to this novel method of payment: the near-bankrupt Directory could not have afforded the sort of victory promised by Fulton. A ship-of-the-line like HMS *Victory* would have cost 400,000 francs, equivalent to a cool million pounds or more in modern terms. Even a modest run of successes would have brought France to her knees, and the Directory started to haggle over the price. They cut the size of Fulton's remuneration, and on the advice of the Minister of Marine, refused to grant commissions or letters-of-marque to the crews of submarines, thus ensuring that the British would hang them as pirates.

Disgusted, Fulton took his ideas to Holland, but the thrifty burghers were even less inclined to invest in his project. Two years later he found himself back in Paris, but this time he was dealing with the dynamic First Consul, Napoleon Bonaparte, not a committee of nonentities. Napoleon, desperate to launch an invasion of England, was eager to find any way of defeating British seapower, and authorised the payment of 10,000 francs to Fulton to allow him to build the submarine.

Work began in the winter of 1799, and the following spring the boat was ready for launch as the *Nautilus*, a name which was to make submarine history again a century and

Left: *A modern reconstruction of Bushnell's* Turtle, *based on work done by the Smithsonian Institution.* (SMM)

Right: *Robert Fulton's* Nautilus, *complete with sail to ease the workload on the operator. Although not shown, the explosive charge was towed astern.* (SMM)

a half later. She was cylindrical, with a copper hull on iron frames; like a modern submarine she also had a conning tower and diving planes. Much larger than the *Turtle*, she was manned by a crew of three, and carried a detachable charge for fixing to an enemy ship's hull. First trials were carried out in the River Seine, opposite the Hôtel des Invalides, and Fulton took her down to 25ft.

After such a promising start the *Nautilus* ran into problems. The Maritime Prefect at Brest refused to grant commissions for what he regarded as an inhuman method of waging war. Fulton became embroiled in a series of claims and counter-claims regarding alleged attacks on British ships, and it is small wonder that the French started to label him *le charlatan Americain*. Finally he swallowed his principles and crossed the Channel in 1804 to present his invention to William Pitt, the British Prime Minister. Despite a convincing demonstration when a brig was blown up off Walmer and the support of two brilliant yet maverick Royal Navy officers, Sir Sidney Smith and Sir Home Riggs Popham, the Admiralty wanted nothing to do with the *Nautilus*. The formidable sailor Lord St Vincent said, that Pitt was 'the greatest fool that ever existed to encourage a mode of warfare which those who commanded the sea did not want, and which, if successful, would deprive them of it'. This put-down has been condemned as reactionary and stupid, but St Vincent was right. The submarine was nowhere near ready to take its place in any navy. With nothing but muscle-power and only the crudest of close-range weapons, it was still nothing more than a toy.

When Napoleon was defeated at Waterloo on 18 June 1815 and sent into exile a second time, a period of relative peace and stability in Europe ensued. Reflecting this, submarine inventors seem to have lain low for nearly half a century. In 1850, however, war broke out between Prussia and Denmark. The powerful Danish fleet blockaded the coast of Prussia, and for much the same reason that Bushnell and Fulton had turned to submarine design, a Bavarian artillery sergeant called Wilhelm Bauer produced an idea for driving off the Danish ships. His submarine was called the *Brandtaucher* or 'Fire Diver', virtually a sheet-iron rectangular tank driven by a handwheel. Water ballast was admitted to destroy buoyancy, but the diving angle was altered by winding a heavy weight forwards and backwards.

The principal failing of the *Brandtaucher* was her rectangular box form, which was not ideal for structural strength. Her first voyage in December 1850 was a success, and forced the Danish fleet to withdraw, but little more than a month later she suffered a disastrous accident in Kiel harbour. The plating at the stern collapsed under the pressure of 50ft (16 metres) of water, trapping Bauer and his crew. Bauer kept a clear head, and persuaded his two sailors to allow the boat to flood, to equalise pressure to the point where they could open a hatch. The two sailors were understandably panicky, but after a desperate argument Bauer won them round, and after five hours they were able to reach the surface, the first submariners to escape from a damaged submarine.

Bauer was not discouraged, and after some unsuccessful attempts to sell his ideas he went to Britain. The Crimean War, 1854-56, had begun and Prince Albert introduced the Bavarian to high-ranking naval officers to see if there was a way of attacking the Russian fleets. What followed is a great mystery; Lord Palmerston sanctioned the expenditure of £7000 and Bauer was told to discuss technical details with the distinguished naval architect Scott Russell. Admiral Sir Astley Cooper-Key remembered seeing 'Lord Palmerston's Submarine' as no more than a large diving bell 'capable of accommodating two men', but this does not sound like any of Bauer's known designs. The Victorians were obsessed by technical progress, and yet there is no record of the design, the Liverpool shipyard, or *any* contractual details in official Admiralty records. The likeliest explanation seems to be that Palmerston allowed false details to leak out, to alarm the Russians.

Like other submarine salesmen, Bauer had no compunction in changing sides, and in 1855 he was talking to the Russians. He was allowed to build the 52ft (17 metres) *Seeteufel* ('Sea Devil'), sometimes referred to as *le Diable Marin*. On 6 September 1856, to celebrate the coronation of Czar Alexander II, the *Seeteufel* embarked a group of musicians, who, if Russian claims are to be believed, struck up 'God Preserve the Czar' while travelling submerged (probably awash) off Kronstadt. Whatever else this piece of showmanship achieved, it showed how far sound can travel underwater.

As soon as the Russians sued for peace in 1856, the temporary alliance between Britain and France lapsed. Anglo-French rivalry took up where it had left off, and in 1858 the Minister of Marine called for proposals to design a submersible to protect France's coasts. A Captain Bourgois presented an acceptable design for a 140ft (46 metres) boat, and five yeas later the *Plongeur* was launched at Rochefort. The upsurge in naval technology, hastened by the recent war, was beginning to take effect, and the *Plongeur* had 23 reservoirs for compressed air, and a 4-cylinder engine. In practice the reservoirs could not be filled to any significant pressure-level, so blowing the tanks took some time, and the age-old problem of weaponry was still not solved. The *Plongeur* was armed with a 'spar torpedo', a canister of gunpowder on the end of a pole, a *kamikaze* weapon which would virtually guarantee destruction of the attacker. She never had a chance to demonstrate her limited capabilities, and she was disarmed in 1867 and later converted to a surface torpedo boat. Amazingly, in her new guise she survived until 1937, although only a hulk by then.

The American Civil War, 1861-65, witnessed major advances in the concept of under-water warfare. Once again, the weaker power, in this case the Confederate States, needed to break the Union Navy's blockade of its ports, to allow the export of cotton to European markets. Using its limited resources the Confederate Navy developed semi-submersible spar torpedo boats, known as 'Davids' because they were pitted against the Yankee 'Goliaths', but they were not submarines, merely steam torpedo boats using water ballast to reduce the silhouette. In conjunction, however, the Confederacy was working on fully submersible vessels, and in 1862 the *Pioneer* was built at New Orleans. She had to be scuttled to prevent capture by Union forces, but the wreck was later salvaged and preserved in the Louisiana State Museum. Better known was a submersible designed by Horace L Hunley and built by James R McLintock at Mobile, Alabama. She was cylindrical, fabricated from .375in boiler plate, had a 42in diameter hull, and was propelled by an eight-man hand crank.

Unfortunately she was lethally unsafe. Swamped by the wash of passing steamers she sank three times yet on each occasion was raised. In all she drowned 23 men, including her designer. In early 1864, renamed the CSS *Hunley* after her late inventor, she was prepared for a last desperate attack on the Union blockade of Charleston harbour. By this time the Navy had lost much of its enthusiasm for the *Hunley*, and there was no inter-service rivalry to block an offer from the 21st Regiment of the Alabama Light Infantry to provide a fourth crew. These eight brave men, under Lieutenant George E Dixon, were offered a huge reward for risking their lives in the boat, and set out from Charleston on the evening of 17 February 1864. Dixon sighted the steam frigate USS *Housatonic* in the distance, and steered towards her. A little before 8.45pm the *Housatonic*'s Officer of the Deck spotted what appeared to be a piece of driftwood or a tree trunk approaching the ship, and he ordered the ship to Beat to Quarters. But it was too late, and the 143lb gunpowder charge on its 30ft pole detonated with a tremendous explosion, blowing a

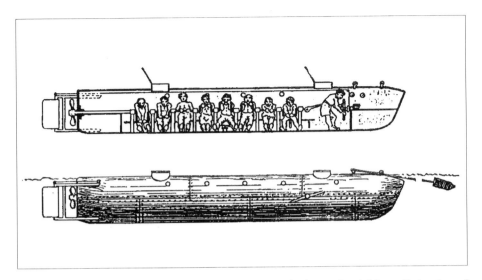

huge hole in the frigate's starboard side. *Housatonic* had won the dubious distinction of being the first ship to be sunk by a submarine.

For some time it was thought that the *Hunley* had somehow escaped, but many years later she was discovered lying alongside her victim, with eight skeletons seated at the hand crank. Initially it was thought that she was swamped by the blast, but in fact it is now believed that she was sucked into the huge hole in the *Housatonic*'s hull. If there had been a way to detonate the spar torpedo from inside the boat, Dixon would not have left the forward hatch open, and he and his men might have lived to earn their reward.

The exploit of the *Hunley* created enormous interest in submersibles and, as was to be expected, several dubious ideas were proposed. Among them were a M. Villeroi's *Alligator* and Oliver Halstead's *Intelligent Whale*, which can be seen in the grounds of the Washington Navy Museum. The latter eclipsed the *Hunley* in killing 39 people during trials, but thereafter she lapsed into obscurity. In 1994 the wreck of the *Hunley* was relocated in Charleston harbour, and she is now being restored as a monument to the Confederate States Navy.

On both sides of the Atlantic the potential of the submarine was now recognised, but even more important, technology was developing fast, and promised to solve some of the problems which had hamstrung earlier inventors. On the Adriatic at Fiume in 1866 an English engineer, Robert Whitehead, was developing a novel idea for a mechanical wire-guided explosive fish tried out by a retired Austro-Hungarian Army officer, Captain Luppis (also rendered di Luppi). Whitehead abandoned the steering wires, and devised an 'automobile' vehicle capable of running below the surface, and mindful of the term 'torpedo' used to describe Confederate moored mines, called his invention the 'fish' torpedo. In fact the name torpedo derives from an electric ray which stuns its prey. Here at last was a means of attacking a hostile ship from a (relatively) safe distance. The Royal Navy reacted swiftly by buying the rights to the 'Whitehead Secret', a hydrostatic valve to ensure a constant running-depth, before it had a vessel capable of launching the weapon. By the late 1870s Whitehead's factory was turning out torpedoes and other countries were copying them (the German Schwartzkopf design was pure coincidence, not flagrant industrial espionage).

The Imperial Russian Navy built the so-called *Aleksandrovski* type submarine, a 355-ton boat with a length of 110ft (33.5 metres) driven by a compressed air engine, at St

Petersburg in the 1860s. Her advanced features and size showed great promise, but her hull was crushed while diving to a depth of 100ft (over 40 metres) in 1871. The next experiment went to the other extreme, 52 15ft (4.5-metre) boats built to the design of the Polish engineer Stefan Drzewiecki. The design was developed into two large types, all treadle-driven, and they were intended to lay two dynamite mines each. All were deleted in 1886 and converted to harbour craft. Drzewiecki has one other claim to fame, his 'drop collar' method of launching torpedoes. The Royal Navy used these devices only in small torpedo boats, but French submarine-designers incorporated them in designs built up to the First World War.

In England, the Reverend George Garrett was influenced by events in the Russo-Turkish War of 1877, and envisaged a submarine capable of carrying out peaceful tasks, such as removing 'torpedoes' (i.e. mines) and underwater surveying. In 1878 he floated a company to build his first boat, the first *Resurgam* ('I will rise again'). She was tiny, 14ft (4.3 metres) long and 5ft (1.5 metres) in diameter. She was hand-cranked but revived an old idea, a piston to vary the displacement for diving and surfacing, and would in theory be able to attach explosive charges to a target's hull. Encouraged by the trials, the following year Garrett decided to build a larger, steam-powered boat, *Resurgam II*. She displaced about 30 tons, and had a Lamm 'fireless locomotive' engine, similar to those used on London's underground railways. This stored steam under pressure, which released latent heat to create fresh steam to drive a reciprocating engine. Unfortunately she was lost in 1880 while in tow off the Welsh coast, where the wreck has been discovered, but she is in a poor state, and salvage is unlikely.

In the nick of time Garrett's promising enterprise was saved by the Swedish arms manufacturer Thorsten Nordenfelt, who injected fresh capital and hired Garrett to supervise the construction of a new submarine, the *Nordenfelt No. 1*. She was sold to Greece in 1883, stirring Turkey to buy another two in 1886, the *Abdul Medjid* and *Abdul Hamid*. None of these was a success, for like all the early experimental craft, they lacked longitudinal stability, and there was a dearth of volunteers willing to risk their lives in such unpredictable vessels. They were, however, a major advance in that they were the first to be armed with the 14in Whitehead torpedo. The Greek boat was scrapped about 1901, never having been operational, but the Turkish pair were found by the Germans in 1914, abandoned in a shed in the Arsenal at Constantinople. Hopes of refitting them for harbour defence were dashed when it was found that the hulls were too badly corroded.

The giant *Nordenfelt IV* was built at Barrow in 1887 for Russia, displacing 245 tons submerged, with a length of 125ft (38.4 metres). She appeared at the Golden Jubilee Fleet Review, despite having encountered severe problems on trials. In November 1888 she set

One of two Nordenfelt boats built at Chertsey for the Imperial Ottoman Navy. Note the hump covering the bow torpedo-tube, the tall funnel, the Nordenefelt machine gun, and the totally ineffective vertical propellers.
(BAES Marine)

sail for Kronstadt, but was wrecked on the Jutland coast of Denmark. Although raised only two weeks later, the Russian Government refused to pay for her, and this proved the last straw for Nordenfelt. He dissolved the partnership, leaving Garrett to emigrate to the United States and die in poverty in 1902.

A young Spanish naval officer, Lieutenant Isaac Peral y Caballero, solved the next major problem, finding a propulsion system that was not dependent on oxygen. He was not the first to think about electric propulsion, but generators and accumulator batteries were very heavy. Peral decided to drive his 87-ton boat with two 30 horsepower motors drawing current from a 420-cell battery. He also remembered the purpose of a submarine, and included a launch-tube for three Schwartzkopf torpedoes. The submarine, named *Peral* in honour of his achievement, was built at Cadiz in 1887-1890 and after being paid off early in the last century, was preserved as a memorial.

The Spanish Navy lacked the financial resources to exploit Peral's design, but the French had already grasped the potential of battery-power. French industry had made good progress in electrical engineering, and the distinguished naval architect Dupuy de Lôme started work on a design of his own. On his death in 1885 his disciple Gustave Zédé took over, and by November 1886 the Ministry of Marine was ready to place an order. Details had to be worked out, and the new boat, known as the *Gymnote* ('Eel') was not laid down until April 1887, and did not start trials for another 18 months. She was never meant to be more than a test-bed, and during the next decade she was twice rebuilt. She had no generator, and relied entirely on a 564-cell accumulator battery, coming alongside a depot ship or pier to recharge. The next boat was much larger, and although she was not trouble-free, she convinced the Navy that submarines were worth developing. Originally to be named *Sirène*, she was renamed *Gustave Zédé* in honour of her designer, who had died during her construction.

In February 1896 the French Minister of Marine, M. Lockroy, proposed an open competition to produce designs for a 200-ton craft with a range of 100 miles on the surface. No fewer than 29 designs were submitted from all over the world, the winner being Maxime Laubeuf. He deserves the credit for finally solving the basic problems of submarine propulsion. His remarkable *Nautilus* had two propulsion systems, a 220 horsepower steam engine for surface-running, and an 80 horsepower electric motor for submerged power. Laubeuf's refinement was to make the steam engine run a dynamo to charge the accumulator battery, giving her a far greater range than the all-electric boats. To distinguish her from these boats, she was classified as a *submersible*, as against the electric *sousmarins*. This distinction still causes confusion, because today's submarines reverse this, with diesel-electric boats being referred to as submersibles and nuclear boats being regarded as 'true' submarines. In reality the *Nautilus* was a submersible torpedo boat, intended to use her steam plant to reach her operational area, and then dive to attack targets, a tactic which was to become standard for the next half century.

British inventors had been seized with the same enthusiasm. The ones who came closest to winning official acceptance were Ash and Campbell, who in 1888 built a 50-ton boat powered by twin Edison-Hopkins electric motors using current from two 52-cell batteries. She was named *Nautilus* in honour of Fulton's boat, and a number of dignitaries were invited to witness a diving trial at Tilbury, including Admiral Lord Charles Beresford and Sir William White, Director of Naval Construction, 1885-1901. Unfortunately she dived into the mud at the bottom of the dock and remained stuck for over an hour, and only worked herself free when the people on board rushed backwards and forwards to break the suction. Mr Waddington's *Porpoise* of 1892 was soundly engineered but failed to attract financial backing.

In the United States a fiercely fought competition between John P Holland and Simon Lake would decide who won a coveted US Navy contract. Holland had been experimenting with submarine design since the 1870, using funds from the Irish nationalist Fenian Brotherhood, in the hope of destroying British naval supremacy. As time passed Holland became less interested in politics and more concerned with making a living as an engineer.

In 1893 the US Navy announced a competition for a submarine design, and Holland, Lake and Baker submitted bids. Baker's proposals were soon ruled out, and when Lake's prototype could not be completed in time the Bureau of Ordnance awarded the contract to Holland. The boat was to be called the *Plunger*, and was launched in 1897 after a number of changes and delays. So many of the alterations were made without the approval of the designer that he withdrew from the contract, and ordered his Holland Boat Company to build a second boat at its own expense. His confidence was justified, for the *Plunger* totally failed on trials, and she was never accepted. The *Holland*'s trials, by comparison, were a great success, and she was bought by the US Navy for $120,000 in

John P Holland peers out of the hatch of one of his own submarines, accepted by the US Navy after a long and expensive struggle. Within a decade the Electric Boat Company was supplying designs to navies around the world. (SMM)

1900. A year later seven of the improved *Adder* class were under construction, and the Royal Navy had started negotiations to build to Holland's design under licence.

The *Holland* differed from the *Narval* in several ways. She also had a dual propulsion system, but used a 45 horsepower gasoline engine for surface running, giving more power for less weight, and allowing more rapid diving. The hull was spindle-shaped, and instead of a double hull, stowed fuel in 'saddle' tanks outside a single hull. Nor was there any attempt to provide a boat-shape for surface running.

Despite the pioneering work of Bauer, the German Navy showed little initial interest in matching foreign developments. Admiral Tirpitz saw submarines as a threat to his plans for a large surface fleet, and although some early experimental boats were built privately, the Imperial German Navy showed no interest in them. Only when a renegade French designer, M. d'Equevilley, went to work for Krupp's Germania shipyard did the Navy wake up to the developments in other navies, and as a result *U.1* did not enter service until 1906.

As this brief historical outline shows, the Royal Navy did not come to submarines suddenly. In Britain and elsewhere designers had been steadily coming to terms with the problems of submarine design, and learning, sometimes painfully, how to exploit emerging technologies. It had been a long process, and the late nineteenth century pioneers could hardly have imagined how fast submarines would develop in the next decade.

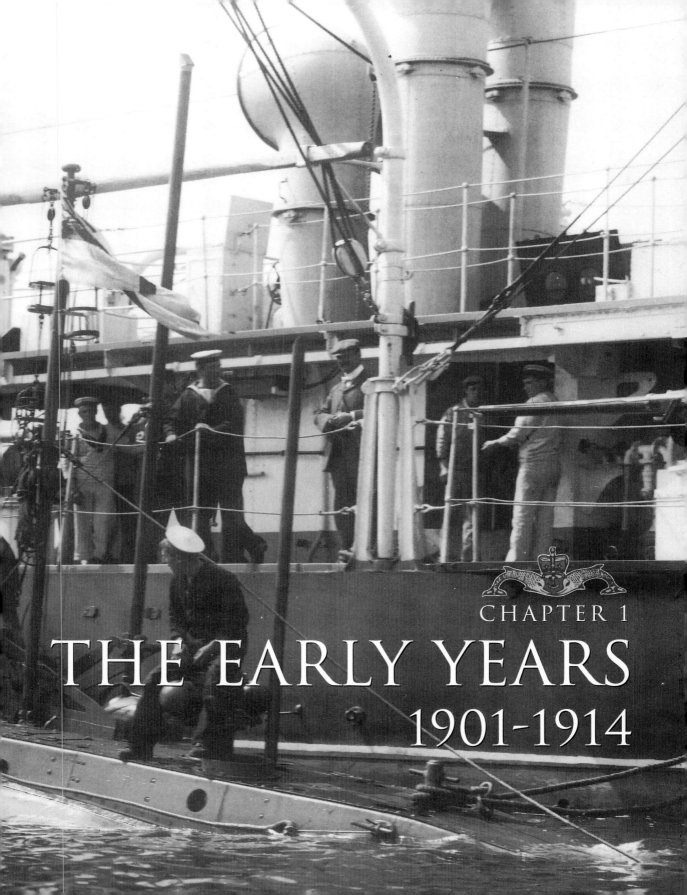

CHAPTER 1

THE EARLY YEARS
1901-1914

IN 1900 THE ROYAL NAVY was at the height of its power, superficially still reflecting the atmosphere of an exclusive yacht club, but in fact innovative and eager to embrace new technology. The long Victorian peace was over, and new threats were emerging. By 1905 the two traditional naval enemies, France and Russia, were in decline. The French Navy had degenerated sharply in efficiency as a result of political meddling. The Imperial Russian Navy had suffered a humiliating defeat at the hands of the Japanese at Tsushima, 27 May 1905. But in their place was Germany. The rising industrial power and wealth of Germany had already created an army second to none. But Kaiser Wilhelm II and Secretary of State for the Navy Admiral Alfred von Tirpitz longed for the prestige of a navy capable of challenging the Royal Navy and securing an overseas empire for the German nation.

Germany's growing naval and military strength created great instability across Europe, principally in France and Russia, even Great Britain belatedly recognised the threat to security of a France under German occupation. German diplomacy, never a strong point, failed to placate its rivals, who created a network of formal and informal mutual security agreements. The French and Russians had been allies for many years, to offset British sea power, but growing Anglo-French fear of Germany led to the *Entente Cordiale* in 1901. The impossible had happened, the British had realised the risks of 'splendid isolation' and had reached agreement with their 'hereditary' enemy, a situation which German foreign policy should never have permitted.

Although the *Entente* was not a military alliance, it should have sounded a warning to Germany that it could no longer count on British neutrality in a future European war. The German public response was instead to agonise about 'encirclement' while its diplomats sought to bind Italy and the Austro-Hungarian Empire to its cause as allies, ignoring the deep animosity between the two Mediterranean neighbours. In contrast, both Britain and France worked hard to restore Russia's defence capability, providing both training and technical help.

Great Britain had been prepared to tolerate German dominance on land secured by the swift victories over Austria in 1866 and France in 1870-71. But the implicit threat of the German Navy Laws passed from the late 1890s onwards finally alerted the nation to the unwelcome news that the Royal Navy's supremacy was being seriously challenged. The result was the Anglo-German naval arms race, incorrectly viewed by many as the cause of the First World War, but in reality only the most obvious symptom of deeper rivalries. The building of the revolutionary battleship HMS *Dreadnought* in 1905 marked the point at which the British flung down the gauntlet, and soon a policy of 'two keels to one' became a feature of naval policy. Great Britain was determined to use its superior industrial resources to outbuild the German Navy.

As fast as relations with Germany deteriorated, those with France improved. The Royal Navy had taken major steps to reduce Imperial strategic overstretch. The Anglo-Japanese Treaty allowed the Navy to maintain only token forces in China, the establishment of the Royal Australian Navy further reduced the burden of policing the Pacific, and, in a return to traditional naval policy, major modern warships were brought home to concentrate power in the Channel and the North Sea. The French Navy was persuaded to allow the Royal Navy to shoulder the burden of defending Northern France against German attack, while it concentrated its forces in the Mediterranean.

British war plans focused on a possible 'bolt from the blue', with the German High Seas Fleet using torpedo boats and submarines in surprise attacks. In German military theory such an onslaught would inflict losses on the British battle fleet, reducing it to parity and creating ideal conditions for the High Seas Fleet to engage on roughly equal terms. Alternatively, the German high command was credited with the ability to carry out

Previous page:
The Hollands *were so
small that they were even
dwarfed by the small
torpedo gunboat HMS*
Hazard. (SMM)

24

amphibious landings, exemplified by the plot of *The Riddle of the Sands*. Such an attack would be helped by an estimated 80,000 German army reservists masquerading as hairdressers and musicians throughout the country, and using pre-positioned arms dumps. Time was to show that Germany's leaders were far too cautious for such bold plans, and the Navy certainly lacked any sort of amphibious warfare doctrine. Not that the Royal Navy had given much thought to such operations either, being content to escort an expeditionary force to France, using commandeered North Sea and Channel passenger ferries.

'A fish out of water', one of the Hollands *being moved by the hammerhead crane at Vickers' Barrow yard.* (Author's collection)

Meanwhile the Royal Navy was in a ferment of modernisation, under the dynamic leadership of Sir John Fisher, the First Sea Lord. Advances in weaponry and engineering rendered many of the Victorian warships obsolescent, and created a demand for new tactics. On the debit side, it also reduced the huge margin of numbers enjoyed by the Royal Navy over it rivals, forcing it to compete with the Germans solely in terms of new ships. However, the benefits far outweighed the disadvantages, and pre-empted any possibility of Germany producing a sudden technological advantage. Steam turbines replaced reciprocating engines, oil fuel replaced coal, and overall reliability improved. In particular, the torpedo made the transition from an unreliable 'toy' to a lethal, long-range ship-killer, and the mine proved its worth in the Russo-Japanese War by inflicting heavy casualties on both sides.

The one serious weakness of the Edwardian Navy was the lack of a Naval Staff. Fisher could not see the need for one, fearing that it would limit his freedom of action. Not until 1911 was there a showdown between the politicians and the admirals, when the new First Lord of the Admiralty, Winston Churchill, was ordered to create a staff organisation from nothing, capable of evaluating peacetime experience and planning systematically for war. Some inroads were made in the education of naval officers at the Royal Naval College, Greenwich, but war experience was to show that the time was too short to create an efficient Naval Staff.

At a time of such rapid technical advance in ship-design, weaponry and tactics, it was inevitable that the Royal Navy should turn its attention to the submarine. Inventors had dreamt of submarines for four centuries, and several faltering steps had been taken by such visionary pioneers as Bushnell, Fulton Bourne and Bauer. By the end of the nineteenth century, relatively large numbers of submarines had been built, primarily by the Russian and French navies, but they were dangerous to operate and very limited in their operational offensive potential.

The Royal Navy recognised that the submarine was a viable proposition, it did not appear in the navy by some spark of sudden genius. With rapid progress being made in France and the United States, the Admiralty could not afford to ignore the new technology. Contrary to popular mythology, there was a strong lobby in the upper echelons of the Navy in favour of an investigation into the feasibility of 'submarine boats'. Indeed, Sir William White, DNC had went so far as to dive in the experimental submarine *Nautilus*, although the experience left him shaken but not stirred when the boat had embedded herself in mud for some time.

In the late 1890s Sir William urged the Admiralty to build its own prototype or to purchase the best foreign design. As a result, negotiations started with the Electric Boat Company in 1900, resulting in the purchase of a licence to build a Holland design similar to those coming into service with the US Navy. Although Admiral Sir Arthur Wilson VC is always quoted as saying that submarines were, 'Underhand and damned un-English' and recommending the hanging of their crews as pirates, there is no record of this ever being said or written. As one of the Navy's top technical specialists he was, moreover, responsible for recommending the purchase of a reliable design.

Despite the fact that the purchase was published in the Naval Estimates, the Admiralty hoped to keep the existence of the Holland boats secret, so secret that very few senior officers were aware of their existence for some years. This may account for the popular myth of the Navy taking no interest in submarines, but it actually underlines how seriously the Royal Navy took the potential of the new weapon.

Progress in the new submarine branch was rapid, not least because the small number of personnel created a close-knit 'family' organisation with excellent morale. After the

Holland No.*1 afloat at last, on 2 October 1901 at Barrow.* (BAES Marine)

Hollands, only three classes of coastal submarines were built before the diesel-engined patrol type appeared. Given the advanced technology involved, the transition from experimental boats to reliable weapons of war in less than 14 years was remarkable. The last pre-war design stood the test of wartime operations extremely well, and remained in front-line service to the end of hostilities, testimony to the soundness of pre-war procurement policy.

When war finally came in the summer of 1914, the Royal Navy was not caught in any of the fiendish traps that pre-war theorists had envisaged. There was no 'secret army' of German troops in the country, and German espionage was no more than a minor irritant. Quite fortuitously, a full-scale Fleet Mobilisation had been planned for July, with the result that every ship capable of putting to sea was manned and brought to full readiness. The mobilisation was a great success, and was followed by a huge Fleet Review in Spithead. Thereafter the ships were intended to disperse back to their peacetime stations or return to the Reserve Fleet, but the brash young First Lord of the Admiralty sensed that the political crisis in the Balkans would worsen. On his own initiative Churchill cancelled the dispersal order, and as a precaution ordered the crews to remain with their ships in expectation of an order to send the ships to their war stations. In his own words, there were no torpedo boats appearing out of the mists of the North Sea, and no raid by the German battle fleet, but the Royal Navy was fully prepared for any eventuality.

mid-December 1900	Agreement signed with Electric Boat Co. for five Holland Type X submarines to be built by Vickers Sons & Maxim at Barrow in Furness.
4 February 1901	Holland *Submarine No.1* laid down at Barrow in Furness.
2 October 1901	*Submarine No.1* launched

The *Holland* class

Displacement:	113/122 tons
Dimensions:	63ft 10in (oa) x 11ft 10in x 9ft 11in
Machinery:	single-shaft 4-cylinder Wolseley petrol engine, 1 electric motor, 160/70hp
Speed:	7.5/6kts
Range:	500nm at 7kts
Armament:	1-18in TT (bow), 3 torpedoes
Complement:	8

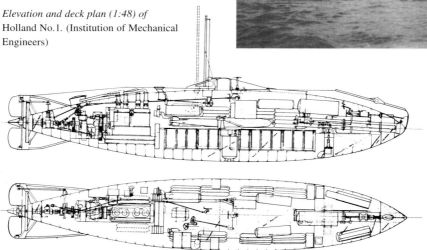

Elevation and deck plan (1:48) of Holland No.1. *(Institution of Mechanical Engineers)*

HM Submarine Holland No.1 *under way in Spithead. The low freeboard of the Hollands made them vulnerable to being swamped by waves and the wakes of passing ships. (SMM)*

The crew of Holland No.3 *pose for a group photograph. The small crews and the even smaller number of boats combined to make service in submarines a 'family business', something which persists in today's world. (SMM)*

Holland No.5, *showing the binnacle aft (a magnetic compass did not work inside the hull), and a rating at the surface steering position forward of the vestigial conning tower. The ship in the background appears to be* HMS Hazard. *(SMM)*

Captain Bacon, Father of the Submarine Service

The decision to appoint Captain Reginald Hugh Spencer Bacon as Inspecting Captain of Submarine Boats in 1901 was an inspired choice. Not only was he one of the foremost technical specialists in the Navy, he had specialised in torpedo work as a lieutenant, but also a forceful personality who threw himself into the job with great enthusiasm. His style was what might today be called 'confrontational', and he did not suffer fools gladly, but he fought the submariners' corner with conspicuous success. During Fisher's great naval reforms of 1904-10 Bacon would be one of the most influential members of the 'Fishpond'.

Bacon did not victimise submariners who made mistakes, but he insisted that practical lessons must be learned from them. One of his unorthodox methods was to give erring officers the 'Black Spot' if they made a serious mistake or suffered an accident, but it was promptly passed to the officer who made the next mistake. One of his disconcerting tricks was to insist on taking charge of vessels, and several accidents occurred, but his subordinates knew that he would never order them to do anything that he had not tried himself.

Captain Reginald Bacon RN proved the ideal officer to run the new Submarine Service. With a good grasp of technical matters, a 'can do' outlook, and a willingness to experience problems at first hand, he enthused the early submariners and pushed them to a high standard of efficiency. (SMM)

15 January 1902 First surface run of *Holland No.1* using the gasoline engine.

20 March 1902 First dive of *Holland No.1* in the basin at Barrow, slung on chains for safety. The first free dive took place three days later.

Summer 1902 1st Submarine Flotilla (*Submarines 2* and *3*, escorted by the torpedo gunboat *Hazard* and *TB.42*) left Barrow for Portsmouth, where they were subsequently joined by Nos.*1*, *4* and *5*. When *No.4* was off Holyhead the tow was slipped, and the escorts were alarmed to get no response to signals or hails. When they came alongside, they found the crew asleep, having been working all night under very difficult conditions.

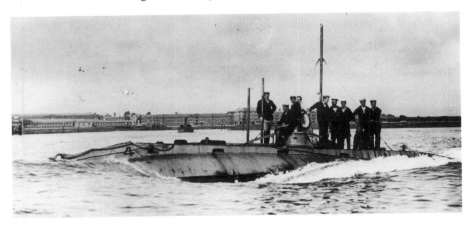

Even in smooth water Holland No.4 *creates a wave capable of sinking her if anyone becomes careless.* (SMM)

*The launch of A.1 at
Barrow on 16 April 1903.
She was the first British-
designed submarine to be
built, but she would
become the Royal Navy's
first submarine casualty
only 11 months later.*
(SMM)

*A.3 seen some time
between her completion
in 1903 and her loss in
1912. The bands on the
conning tower are
unusual, as other
photographs show her
with the number 13
painted up (indicating
flotilla, as well as the
individual boat).*
(BAES Marine)

16 April 1903   *A.1* launched at Barrow in Furness, the first British-designed and built submarine. *A1-13* built 1902-1905.

18 March 1904   The Royal Navy's first submarine lost, when *A.1* was rammed and sunk by the liner SS *Berwick Castle* in the Solent, during exercises. Her commanding officer (CO), Lt Mansergh, and all ten of her complement died. It is assumed that Mansergh was so intent on firing a practice torpedo that he failed to see or hear the liner approaching astern. *A.1* was raised a month later and scrapped.

The most noticeable improvement visible in A.2 and her sisters was the provision of a proper conning tower, with a small compass platform. This improved safety when running on the surface, and there were many internal improvements. (SMM)

The 'A' class

A planned improvement, *Holland No.6*, incorporated so many changes that she became the first of the new 'A' class, the first British-designed boats. They showed many improvements over the Electric Boat design, notably a proper conning tower, and *A.13* was the first to be driven by a diesel engine.

'A' class Specifications

Displacement:	190/205-207 tons
Dimensions:	*A.1* 103ft 3in (oa) x 11ft 10in x 10ft 1in.
	A.2-13 105ft .5in (oa) x 12ft 8.75in x 10ft 8in
Machinery:	*A.1-12* single-shaft 16-cyl Wolsely petrol engine, 1 electric motor, 350-550/125-150hp
	A.13 single-shaft Hornsby-Ackroyd 6-cyl heavy oil (diesel) engine, 1 electric motor, 500/150hp
Speed:	*A.1-12* 10-11.5/6-7kts.
	A.13 11/6kts
Range:	320nm at 7kts
Armament:	*A.1-4* 1-18in TT (bow), 3 torpedoes.
	A.5-13 2-18in TT (bow), 4 torpedoes
Complement:	11

A.1 in Portsmouth Harbour during 1903.
(Author's collection)

25 October 1904	*B.1* launched at Barrow in Furness. *B.1-11* built 1904-06.
18 April 1905	Launch of *A.13* at Barrow in Furness, the RN's first diesel-engined submarine.
16 June 1905	*A.5* sunk by an explosion of petrol vapour while exercising in Plymouth Sound. The CO, Lt Candy, and three of his company were the only survivors. The wreck was raised four days later and scrapped.

B.6 and her sisters could be distinguished by the diving planes forward of the conning tower, and they were bigger than their predecessors, but were otherwise similar to the 'A' class. (SMM)

The 'B' class

The successors to the 'A' class were very similar but were given a more substantial deck casing to provide a bigger reserve of buoyancy and improve performance on the surface. They were also given a pair of diving planes at the forward end of the conning tower to improve underwater handling. This innovation was not repeated in later designs, but half a century later it appeared in US Navy submarines.

The six boats sent to the Mediterranean, *B.6-11*, were ineffective after the autumn of 1915 through lack of spares, so an arrangement was made with the Italian Navy to convert them to small surface patrol craft at Venice in 1917. This involved removal of the electric motor and batteries, and building a short forecastle with a small wheelhouse and a platform for a 12pdr gun. There is no evidence that the torpedo-tubes were retained. Renumbered *S.6-11*, the five survivors were sold at Malta in 1919 for scrapping.

'B' class specifications

Displacement:	287/316 tons
Dimensions:	142ft 2.5in (oa) x 13ft 7in x 11ft 7in
Machinery:	single-shaft Vickers petrol engine, 1 electric motor, 600/290hp
Speed:	12/6kts
Range:	1000nm at 8.75kts
Armament:	2-18in TT (bow), 4 torpedoes
Complement:	15

A.13 looks no different from the rest of the 'A' class but she had the first 'heavy oil' (diesel) engine in a Royal Navy submarine. (SMM)

16 October 1905   *A.4* (Lt Nasmith), suffered a diving accident, but came to the surface, and then sank while in tow that evening. Raised, she survived until 1920. Earlier that year, while conducting trials with underwater signalling, was swamped by the wash of a passing steamer. Only the presence of mind of her First Lieutenant, Lt Herbert, saved the crew from drowning, and she came to the surface.

The Age of White Mice

The greatest risk to submariners in early vessels was from petrol vapour, not only highly inflammable but also toxic. White mice are more rapid in their reaction to such toxicity, and small cages were provided to warn the crew if the concentration of vapour was dangerous. If the mice 'turned up their toes' it was time to get some fresh air into the boat.

The scheme was never a great success because submariners were too fond of the mice, and they were carefully kept away from sources of fumes. Many were given away to friends on shore to ensure a longer and happier life. Every mouse was listed as Admiralty property, and there seems little doubt that the mortality-rate was exaggerated to conceal the 'deserters'.

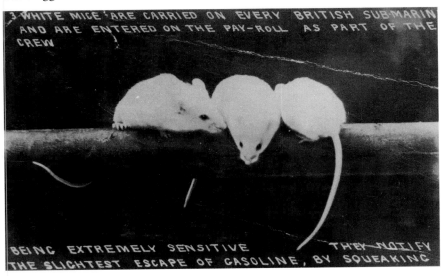

It is easy to understand why early submariners were so fond of the white mice supplied to give warning of carbon monoxide not petrol vapour as the original caption suggests. Many were officially listed as dead, but found their way ashore, to spend their lives as pampered pets. (SMM)

C.17 under way in Spithead, c1908. The canvas 'dodger' provides some protection from spray, but would be useless in bad weather. (BAES Marine)

The 'C' class

With three classes of submarine built, the Admiralty felt confident enough to embark on large-scale production. It is arguable that the construction of nearly 40 coastal boats delayed the introduction of larger 'overseas' patrol submarines, but in spite of their short range and lack of internal space, the 'Cs' saw continuous war service in a number of theatres.

The design was very similar to the 'B' class, with the diving planes removed from the conning tower. Some were camouflaged late in the war.

'C' class Specifications

Displacement:	287-290/316-320 tons
Dimensions:	142ft 2.5in (oa) x 13ft 7in x 11ft 2in-11ft 6in
Machinery:	single-shaft 16-cyl Vickers petrol engine, 1 electric motor, 600/300hp
Speed:	13/7.5kts
Range:	1000nm at 8.75kts
Armament:	2-18in TT (bow), 4 torpedoes
Complement:	16

C.24 puts to sea from Barrow. Despite her small size, she embodies the submarine as we know it. (BAES Marine)

10 July 1906   *C.1-2* launched at Barrow in Furness. *C1-34* built 1906-10.

16 May 1908   *D.1* launched at Barrow in Furness. *D1-8* built 1907-11, the first class designed for diesel engines.

14 July 1909   *C.11* sunk in collision with the SS *Eddystone* NW of the Haisborough Light, off Cromer. Only two survivors were rescued, the CO Lt Brodie and AB Stripes.

A clutch of 'Cs', almost certainly at Barrow during final completion in 1906 or early 1907. Left to right: C.23, unidentified, C.24 and C.21. (BAES Marine)

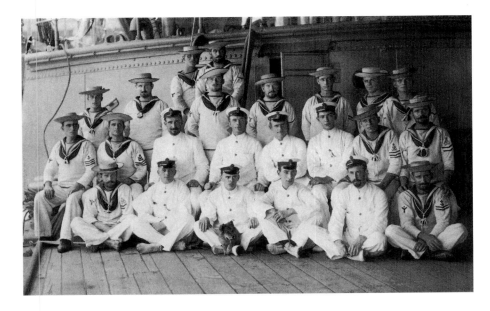

A group of engine room artificers (ERAs) and ratings from the three 'C' class boats on the China Station. Some are wearing the sennet straw hat, which remained in use until after 1918. (SMM)

35

D.2 *off Portsmouth, presumably leaving Fort Blockhouse and swinging to starboard to proceed to Spithead and the open sea. Clearly a pre-war view, with an Isle of Wight steamer and possibly the Royal Yacht* Victoria and Albert *(far left).* (SMM)

The 'D' class

Approved in 1906, these were the first RN submarines capable of extended overseas patrol work, and were also the first class driven by diesel engines (see *A.13*). Most of the improved capabilities were a direct result of increased displacement: more internal volume and a bigger crew reduced the workload on a long patrol. Saddle tanks freed more internal space, and twin screw propulsion provided more manoeuvrability. The 'D' class could also transmit radio messages (previous boats could only receive).

'D' class Specifications

Displacement:	483-495/595-620 tons
Dimensions:	162ft 1in-164ft 7in (oa) x 20ft 5in-20ft 6in x 10ft 5in-11ft 5in
Machinery:	2-shaft 6 cyl diesels, 2 electric motors, 1200/550hp
Speed:	14/9kts
Range:	2500nm at 10kts
Armament:	3-18in TT (2 bow, 1 stern), 6 torpedoes, 1-12pdr gun (D.4 only)
Complement:	25

D.4 was the first Royal Navy submarine to be armed with a deck gun, a 12pdr (3in). The number 74 indicates that she is part of the 7th Submarine Flotilla. Taken between 1911 and 1914. (BAES Marine)

Right from the start British submarine design was thorough. This is an elaborate arrangement for testing the 'A' class hullform at the Admiralty Experiment Works (AEW) at Haslar. (Author's collection)

Holland No.2 *alongside the depot ship* Hazard, *a former torpedo gunboat. The sailors relaxing on the casing give a good idea of how small she was. Second World War midgets were only 13ft shorter.* (SMM)

THE ROYAL NAVY SUBMARINE SERVICE

C.36 *at Hong Kong before the First World War, with a white colour-scheme to reduce the effect of the tropical heat. The three 'C' class boats went to China under their own steam, a longer voyage than any other navy's submarines to date. (SMM)*

1910 During the Annual Manoeuvres *D.1* 'torpedoed' two Blue Fleet cruisers off Colonsay, showing that the new boats could operate at considerable distance from their base at Fort Blockhouse.

1910 Capt Roger John Brownlow Keyes appointed Inspecting Captain of Submarines succeeding Commodore Hall. Keyes inaugurated a period of rapid advances in tactics and equipment.

The little torpedo gunboat HMS Hazard, *before she became the Submarine Service's first depot ship. She was hardly the best choice, but her low freeboard amidships provided good access between her deck and the small early submarines. (SMM)*

B.3, B.4 *and* B.5 *alongside a depot ship, HMS* Forth. *This ex-cruiser and her sister HMS* Thames *supported the submarine flotillas before and during the war.* (SMM)

Commodore Stephen Hall RN, who succeeded Bacon as Inspecting Captain of Submarines in 1904. Hall was influential in formulating a coherent submarine design policy and instigated the purchase of foreign designs to stimulate domestic competition and defined future objectives for the service. (SMM)

February 1911   *C.36* (Lt Herbert), *C.37* (Lt Fenner) *C.38* (Lt Codrington) left on a 10,000-mile voyage to Hong Kong under their own power. This was the first overseas deployment, and proved the capabilities of these small coastal boats.

2 February 1912   *A.3* sunk in collision with HMS *Hazard* off the Isle of Wight, with the loss of all hands. Raised five weeks later and sunk as a gunnery target.

4 October 1912   *B.2* sunk in collision with German liner SS *Amerika* in the English Channel. Her CO, Lt Pulleyne, was the only survivor.

9 November 1912   *E.1* launched at Chatham Dockyard.

8 June 1913   Explosion in *E.5*'s main diesel engines, killing an officer and two ratings.

18 June 1913   Launch of *AE.1* at Barrow, the first submarine built for the Royal Australian Navy. She was followed by *AE.2* a month later and the two were commissioned on 22 February 1914.

10 December 1913   *C.14* (Lt Naper) sunk in collision with *Hopper No.27* in Plymouth Sound. No casualties and the wreck was raised. She was repaired and returned to service.

The 'E' class

For the 1910-11 Programme the Admiralty ordered six improved 'D' class. Although the 'Ds' were very popular, the submarine operators wanted beam increased to allow torpedoes to be fired at beam targets. It was felt that bow-shooting was not yet accurate enough against long-range targets, and beam tubes offered more accuracy in short-range engagements. For the first time two watertight bulkheads were incorporated into the design, improving survivability.

Five of the class had the standard Vickers 4-stroke diesel, but as an experiment *E.3* was given Belgian Carel diesels; these proved a failure, and after trials were replaced by standard engines. When war broke out, *E.7* and *E.8* were ordered to the same design, rather than the improved 'E' design already on the drawing board. The design went through many detail changes, and the 'E' class bore the brunt of wartime submarine operations; losses were nearly 50 per cent, but the design formed the basis of the next class.

To save torpedoes in the Sea of Marmora in 1915, *E.7* was given a 6pdr (57mm) gun and *E.2* received a 4in gun.

'E' class Specifications

Displacement:	655/796 tons
Dimensions:	178ft 1in (oa) x 22ft 8.375in x 12ft 6.25in
Machinery:	2-shaft 8 cyl Vickers diesels, 2 electric motors, 1600/840hp
Speed:	15/9kts
Range:	3000nm at 10kts
Armament:	4-18in TT (1 bow, 2 beam, 1 stern), 8 torpedoes
	1-12pdr gun
Complement:	30

E.6 in 1913 or 1914, possibly at the Spithead Review in July 1914. Note the dark grey colour-scheme. (Author's collection)

16 January 1914 *A.7* failed to surface during exercises in Whitsand Bay, with no survivors. Wreck not raised.

28 February 1914 *S.1* launched by Scotts at Greenock, the first of three experimental double-hulled boats built to an Italian Laurenti design. *S.1-3* built 1913-15 and transferred to Italian Navy in October 1915.

23 July 1914 *V.1* launched by Vickers, the first of four experimental double-hulled boats built 1913-15 to a Vickers design.

The old sloop HMS Dolphin, attached to Fort Blockhouse to house submarine crews, around 1908. In her seagoing days she had defended Suakin against Sudanese rebels, and she finished her career attached to the Nautical College at Leith in the 1960s. (SMM)

Experimental Submarines for the Royal Navy

Although submarine design was proceeding along satisfactory lines, with a steady evolution from the original Holland 'spindle' hull to the saddle tank design of the 'E' class, many in the pre-war submarine service felt that there was a risk of the Royal Navy falling behind other navies, and there was an instinctive mistrust of the Vickers monopoly. Commodore Hall therefore sought funds for the construction of a series of experimental designs, some home-grown and others imported, to determine future policy. The original agreement between Vickers and Electric Boat specified that Holland patents could only be used in boats built at Barrow, or in the Royal Dockyards for a premium, of £2500. Vickers tried to demand a royalty of £10,000 on any submarines built in another commercial yard, but the Admiralty refused. No Holland patents were involved in the 'A' design or later designs, but it seems that a similar agreement was drawn up covering these boats, in effect preventing submarines from being built anywhere but Barrow or the dockyards. Two years' notice of cancellation was required, and this was given on 31 March 1911.

Buying a U-boat design from Germany was out of the question, but the French and Italians were helpful, so licences were sought from the Schneider-Laubeuf company in France and the Laurenti company in Italy. Scotts received an order for three Laurenti boats, to be known as the 'S' class, while Armstrong Whitworth received an order for four Schneider-Laubeuf designs, to be known as the 'W' class.

In parallel, Scotts received an order for an experimental steam-driven Laurenti design, to be named *Swordfish*, while Vickers received an order for an ocean-going design, to be named *Nautilus*. Vickers, stung by what the company took as a direct challenge to its competence, demanded the right to build a coastal submarine design to compete against the 'S' and 'W' designs. The company made its case well, and received an order for four 'V' class.

Commodore Hall's policy might have had a very interesting influence on future RN submarines, but the outbreak of war in 1914 wrecked any chance of a measured assessment of the new designs. The 'S' class were ceded to Italy in October 1915 (presumably on the grounds that the Italians would be familiar with the technology). In August 1916 the 'W' class followed. Neither *Swordfish* nor *Nautilus* was successful; the former was converted into a surface patrol vessel, while the latter never became operational, and ended her days charging batteries in Portsmouth Dockyard.

The very 'un-British' appearance of S.1 *betrays the Italian origin of the 'S' class, although they were built at Greenock. Judging by the number of civilians visible she is running trials in the Clyde before handover by Scotts. (SMM)*

Sectional drawing showing the layout of the experimental steam-driven Swordfish. (Denis Griffiths)

steering gear   gun position   condenser   funnel   crew accommodation   gun position

batteries   motor   turbine   boiler room   control room   battery space   beam torpedo tubes

feed water

0 10 20 30 40 50 feet

The large oceangoing prototype HMS Nautilus in 1918, when she had been renamed N.1. She spent most of the war at Portsmouth with the 1st Submarine Flotilla, but was never operational. (SMM)

The 'V' class was the Vickers reply to the foreign 'S' and 'W' designs, built to meet the same requirements. V.1 is seen here in the old Devonshire Dock at Barrow, on completion late in 1914 or early 1915. (SMM)

CHAPTER 2

THE FIRST WORLD WAR

1914-1918

WHEN THE FIRST WORLD WAR erupted across Europe in August and September 1914 the Royal Navy, thanks to the foresight of Churchill, was already at its war stations and the pre-war plans could be immediately implemented. Within a month of the start of the war the whole British Expeditionary Force had been carried to France without the loss of a single soldier. An improvised bombardment force of old battleships and gunboats harried the rapid German advance through Belgium. Although an attempt by the Naval Brigade to hold Antwerp was a failure the operation delayed the German advance and provided allied forces with the time to stabilise a front line in Flanders. However, the main strand of Britain's maritime strategy was the naval blockade of Germany, to prevent vital material and food from being imported.

When the Western Front stabilised in late 1914, not least because both sides were exhausted, the Royal Navy was free to turn its attention to rounding up the small number of German commerce-raiding cruisers operating in the distant oceans, and bringing Imperial troops to Europe. The German East Asiatic Squadron was composed of the armoured cruisers *Scharnhorst* and *Gneisenau* with the light cruisers *Nürnberg*, *Leipzig* and *Dresden*. Under the command of Vice-Admiral Maximilian Graf von Spee, this powerful force scored a quick success over two elderly armoured cruisers, *Good Hope* and *Monmouth*, at the Battle of Coronel, 1 November 1914. Meanwhile, operating independently, SMS *Emden* led a charmed life as a commerce-raider in the Indian and Pacific Oceans. Spee's ships were wiped out at the Battle of the Falklands, 8 December 1914 by the battlecruisers, *Invincible* and *Inflexible* and the smaller cruisers *Kent*, *Cornwall* and *Glasgow*. *Emden* was caught by HMAS *Sydney* whilst trying to cut the international cable link at Cocos-Keeling Island in the Pacific and was intentionally run aground. With the cruiser *Königsberg* trapped in the Rufiji River in East Africa and the *Karlsruhe* sunk by an internal explosion, the surface war was over, and the British Empire's huge mercantile marine had suffered less than 2 per cent losses.

In home waters the peacetime habits of the surface Navy lasted longer than they should have, and the U-boats scored several easy victories. The operational potential of the submarine was brought to the forefront of Royal Navy thinking following the torpedoing of the cruisers *Hogue*, *Cressy* and *Aboukir* off the Dutch coast on 22 September 1914 by the German submarine *U.9*. Within a relatively short space of time the North Sea was filled with minefields by both sides, inhibiting the movements of ships. At Dogger Bank on 24 January 1915 Vice Admiral David Beatty's battlecruiser force encountered and badly mauled a German squadron under the command of Rear Admiral Franz von Hipper. Despite this success it became increasingly clear that there would be no 'second Trafalgar' between the Grand Fleet and the German High Seas Fleet, at least not if the Germans could avoid it. The most the High Sea Fleet could hope for was to trap a small portion of the Grand Fleet, perhaps a single battle squadron, and destroy it before the main force could come to the rescue.

By early 1915 the stalemate on the Western Front had commenced, the High Seas Fleet was avoiding combat and with German commerce wiped from the seas, there were few openings for British offensive operations. It was thus in a mood of strategic frustration that the ill-fated Dardanelles expedition was conceived. Although posterity has damned Winston Churchill for advocating the scheme, he had the support of many of his professional advisers and political colleagues. It was, however, based on a colossal strategic misconception, that the defeat of Turkey would 'knock the props' from under Germany. In reality, Germany was propping up its newest ally, and Turkey's peasant soldiers were to prove doughty fighters. If the Dardanelles expedition had been given the resources it needed, it might still have succeeded, but the heavy losses on the Western

Previous pages:
HM Australian Submarine
AE.2 *arriving at*
Portsmouth on 17
February 1914. She was
lost the following year in
the Sea of Marmora.
(Author's collection)

E.11 returns to Mudros from a successful foray into the Sea of Marmora. Her casing has been painted in an early camouflage pattern.
(SMM)

Front consumed the reinforcements earmarked for Gallipoli. The solitary consolation of the expensive and futile operation was the campaign by Australian, British and French submarines.

The Royal Navy blockade was hurting Germany, and to counter it the U-boats were given permission to wage 'unrestricted' submarine warfare, sinking any merchantman steaming in a 'War Zone' around the British Isles. This proved very unpopular with neutral countries, and the torpedoing of the liner *Lusitania* in April 1915 drew so strong a protest from the US Government that the German Government was forced to overrule the Navy and bring the campaign to an end. The U-boats could continue to sink ships, but only under International Law, which exempted certain categories and required U-boats to stop and search for contraband, and to ensure the safety of the crew.

The Royal Navy drew little satisfaction from the controversial encounter at Jutland on 31 May 1916 fought between Admiral Sir John Jellicoe's Grand Fleet and the High Seas Fleet under the command of Vice Admiral Reinhard Scheer. After accidentally encountering the German fleet Jellicoe failed to score a tactical decisive victory despite crossing the 'T' of the German line of battle. Faults in British ship design and problems with gunnery and armaments combined with signalling errors all contributed to the indecisive nature of the battle. The German fleet managed to escape to the safety of the Heligoland Bight during the night. Although the Germans could congratulate themselves on having lost fewer ships and for getting back to harbour safely, strategically Jutland did nothing to affect the Royal Navy's control of the sea. Moreover, it was now clear to the German command that the High Seas Fleet could not hope to win the naval war. Once again the admirals demanded unrestricted U-boat warfare, convincing themselves that they could ignore the American outrage by bringing the British to their knees before America could come to their rescue.

The plan nearly worked, by early 1917 one in every four merchant ships heading for British ports was being sunk. What averted catastrophe was a series of linked measures. In 1916 the Admiralty had created an ocean salvage force, saving damaged ships so that they could sail once more. Then a massive building programme was initiated to replace lost tonnage, a belated recognition of shipping's role as a national asset. Then the ancient and well-proven measure of commerce-protection, convoy, was introduced in the teeth of opposition from senior officers. One more factor overlooked by the German high command came into play when the United States entered the war: over 1 million tons of German merchantmen lying interned in US ports suddenly became available to the Allies, the equivalent of an instant building programme.

It had been a very near thing, but from late 1917 the collapse of German sea power was rapid. Unable to assume the offensive morale in the High Sea Fleet sagged, leading to serious unrest, and not even the great German land offensive in March 1918 could do more than postpone total collapse. The final act was the refusal of the High Seas Fleet to obey orders, matched by the sudden collapse of the Germany Army, although it must be said that morale in the U-boat Arm never collapsed, despite awful losses in 1917-18. The Russian war-effort had disintegrated in 1918, and exhausted Turkey and Austria-Hungary negotiated separately for peace with the Allies late in 1918.

Despite many frustrations, the Royal Navy had proved equal to the challenge of the worst threat to national survival since the Napoleonic Wars, and its unrelenting pressure on Germany was a major contribution to the victory in November 1918. It had introduced new technology in every field of activity, and the fact that it did not suffer the mutinies which humbled German sea power, proves that its personnel never lost faith in final victory. Nor were the two unrestricted U-boat campaigns able to weaken the morale of merchant seamen, many of them foreign nationals. The Navy had started with a huge industrial advantage, and was able to build and man excellent ships throughout the war.

At the outbreak of war the Royal Navy possessed more submarines than any other navy:

Great Britain	77
France	45
United States	35
Germany	29
Russia	28
Italy	18
Japan	13

Like other navies, the Royal Navy figures included a number of obsolescent craft, and the German Navy, having started late, had a high proportion of modern boats, but these totals give the lie to the myth of the Royal Navy's hostility to submarines. In fact the 'D' and 'E' classes were comparable to the latest in other navies, and in many ways superior.

In the period of escalating tension following the assassination of Archduke Franz Ferdinand in Sarajevo on 28 June 1914, the 'A', 'B' and 'C' class were allocated to the defence of harbours and coastal waters between Plymouth and Dundee. The 8th Flotilla, comprising ten 'Ds' and 'Es', operated separately under Commodore Submarines.

When Fisher returned as First Sea Lord in October 1914, he set about the task of expanding the submarine force with characteristic energy. Unfortunately much of his enthusiasm was misdirected, and he ordered more boats than the Navy could hope to man. In two cases, he awarded contracts to non-specialist yards, which both got into such difficulties that their contracts were cancelled and placed elsewhere. In general, however, the shipbuilding industry responded magnificently, and the real problem soon became one of adequate training, particularly for commanding officers. In fact the prototype of today's 'Perisher' for aspiring COs was not established until 1917.

In 1915 the Submarine Development Committee concluded that six types were needed: coastal, patrol, fleet, cruiser, minelayer and monitor. The cruiser submarine was deferred as there was virtually no German seaborne commerce to attack, and the existing coastal ('F' and 'V' classes), patrol ('E' class) and minelaying (converted 'E' class) were regarded as adequate. The fleet submarine, capable of accompanying the battlefleet, was developed through the 'J' and 'K' classes, and (eventually) the monitor ('M' class).

The Royal Navy's submarines operated in four main theatres, the North Sea, the Baltic, the Dardanelles and the Adriatic. Only in the Dardanelles and the Baltic did it prove possible to wage war against enemy seaborne trade; in the North Sea and to a lesser extent in the Adriatic, the targets were mostly enemy surface ships and submarines. From April 1917 a number of US Navy submarines joined them in the North Sea and North Atlantic. As many of them duplicated Royal Navy submarine numbers, they were distinguished by adding an 'A' to their pendant numbers, for example the USS *L.12* became *AL.12* until the Armistice in 1918.

31 July 1914 The 8th Flotilla under the command of Capt Waistell, arrived at Harwich, its designated war station.

4 August 1914 Governor of British Columbia approves the purchase of Chilean submarines *Iquique* and *Antofagasta* from Seattle Construction Co. to prevent them from falling into German hands. Renamed *CC.1* and *CC.2*, but their temporary distinction of being the only units of British Columbia's navy soon ended, when the Canadian Government bought them for the Royal Canadian Navy.

Below left:
HM Canadian Submarines CC.1 *and* CC.2 *were the first Royal Canadian Navy submarines, and were built in Seattle to a Holland design. They were roughly similar to the 'C' class hence the choice of CC numbers. (SMM)*

Below right:
Members of the crew of the Canadian submarine CC.1, *the former Chilean* Antofagasta, *temporarily taken over in 1914 by the Province of British Columbia, and then handed over to the Royal Canadian Navy. (SMM)*

5 August 1914   At 0300 the Harwich Force sailed, the light cruiser *Attentive* towing *E.6* (Lt Cdr Talbot) and destroyer *Ariel* towing *E.8* (Lt Cdr Goodhart) as far as Teschelling, where the tows were slipped to allow the two submarines to start the first Heligoland Bight patrol.

18 August 1914   *D.2*, *D.3*, *E.5* and *E.7* returned safely from second Heligoland Bight patrol.

21 August 1914   *E.5* (Lt Cdr Herbert) attacked German light cruiser *Rostock* unsuccessfully but the action put an end to a planned raid on the Dogger Bank fishing fleet.

28 August 1914   *E.6* and eight other boats took up positions before the planned raid by surface ships against the German Heligoland Bight patrols. There were several lucky escapes for friendly ships, and unsuccessful attacks on German ships, and *E.4* (Lt Cdr Leir) rescued ten men from destroyer *Defender*'s boats and three German sailors 'as samples'.

13 September 1914   German light cruiser *Hela* torpedoed and sunk off Heligoland by *E.9* (Lt Cdr Max Horton). This was the first sinking of a German warship by a Royal Navy submarine.

Lt Cdr Max Kennedy Horton

Max Horton was the epitome of the submarine CO, aggressive but not reckless, and one who could get the best out of his officers and men. In fact he was the most distinguished submariner in the Royal Navy. As a lieutenant he commanded *Holland No.3*, and by the outbreak of war in 1914 he commanded *E.9*. His sinking of SMS *Hela* in the enemy's 'back yard' in September 1914 earned him early distinction, as the first submarine CO to sink an enemy warship. His account of the event was ribald, for he admitted that one of his officers had a bowel problem, and when he surfaced to rid the boat of the smell, there was the *Hela*. But his greatest achievements were in the Baltic, when his successes in reducing the flow of steel from Sweden to German led to the Germans calling the Baltic *der Hortonsee*.

On his return to England he was given command of the large submarine *J.1*, and then was the first CO of *M.1*. Between the wars he alternated between command at sea and staff appointments ashore, and having achieved the rank of Vice Admiral, commanded the Submarine Service for three years. In November 1942, at the personal behest of Winston Churchill he was appointed Commander in Chief Western Approaches, in charge of the vital war against the U-boats. Max Horton served his country and the Royal Navy with conspicuous success in two world wars.

Max Horton moved from commanding the Royal Navy's submarines to an even more important job, Commander in Chief Western Approaches, fighting the U-boats in the Battle of the Atlantic during the Second World War. (SMM)

Lieutenant Noel Laurence was one of the Submarine Service pioneers. Under his command E.1 *was the first to enter the Baltic in October 1914, and in 1915 torpedoed the battlecruiser* Moltke. *On 5 November 1916, now CO of J.1, he scored a unique 'double', hitting the dreadnoughts* Grosser Kurfurst *and* Kronzprinz, *each with a single torpedo.* (SMM)

A somewhat piratical Lieutenant Maurice Nasmith in the usual submariner's rig of white pullover and seaboots. It is 1907, when he commanded an 'A' boat. (SMM)

19 September 1914   Last sighting of Royal Australian Navy's (RAN) *AE.1* while patrolling St George's Strait off New Britain. Assumed to have struck an underwater obstacle such as a coral reef, she was the first Empire submarine lost in the First World War.

25 September 1914   *E.6* fouled on two mines in Heligoland Bight but escaped.

26 September 1914   *E.1* (Lt Cdr Laurence) and *E.5* (Lt Cdr Benning) reconnoitred Skagerrak as prelude to sending submarines into Baltic.

September 1914   *B.9*, *B.10* and *B.11* sent from Malta to Dardanelles in company with depot ship *Hindu Kush*, to enforce the blockade of the Straits.

6 October 1914   German torpedo boat *S.116* sunk in North Sea by *E.9*.

15 October 1914   *E.1* and *E.9* sail from Gorleston in successful attempt to penetrate the German defences and enter the Baltic. *E.11* (Nasmith) followed two days later, but was forced to turn back by heavy German counter-attacks.

18 October 1914   *E.3* (Lt Cdr Cholmeley) torpedoed by *U.27* while patrolling off the mouth of the Ems River. No survivors.

D.8 (Ltd Cdr Brodie) shadowed German hospital ship *Ophelia*, which was subsequently judged to be 'spying' and interned.

E.1 attacked armoured cruiser *Fürst Bismarck* unsuccessfully in Kiel Bay.

3 November 1914   *D.5* Mined of Gorleston with only five survivors, including her CO Lt Cdr Godfrey Herbert.

early November 1914   Keels of 12 'H' class boats laid at the Fore River Shipyard in Quincy, Massachusetts, to be followed by eight more to be built at the Union Iron Works in San Francisco.

The 'H' Class

In December 1914, as a result of US Government objections about the breach of neutrality, ten were switched to the Canadian Vickers yard in Montreal. *H.1-10* built 1914-15 but delivery of *H.11-20* delayed until US entry into the war in April 1917. *H.13* and *H.16-20* diverted to Chile before delivery, and *H.14-15* became Royal Canadian Navy (RCN) *CH.14-15* in 1919.

'H' Class Specifications

1st and 2nd Groups (*H.1-20*)		3rd Group (*H.21-54*)	
Displacement:	364/434 tons	*Displacement:*	440/500 tons
Dimensions:	150ft (oa) x 15ft 6ins x 12ft 6ins	*Dimensions:*	171ft (oa) x 16ft x 11ft
Machinery:	2-shaft diesels, 2 electric motors, 480/620hp	*Machinery:*	as Groups 1 and 2
Speed:	13/11kts	*Speed:*	13/10.5kts
Range:	1600nm at 10kts	*Range:*	as Groups 1 and 2
Armament:	4-18in TT (bow), 6 torpedoes	*Armament:*	4-21in TT (bow), 6-8 torpedoes 1-3in AA gun
Complement:	22	*Complement:*	22

The first Canadian-assembled 'H' class, H.1, crossed the Atlantic in 1915. It is not clear if this photograph was taken at Halifax, Nova Scotia, or in home waters. (SMM)

'W' Class

W.1 was the first of four experimental boats built 1913-16 to a French Schneider-Laubeuf design. The first pair were built in 15-17 months, a remarkable feat compared to the usual building times. Despite complaints about habitability, their performance was good, with good diving control and efficient venting and flooding systems. All were transferred to Italian Navy in August 1916.

'W' Class Specifications

1st Group (*W.1-2*)

Displacement:	340/500 tons
Dimensions:	171ft 6in (oa) x 15ft 6in x 9ft
Machinery:	2-shaft diesel, electric motors, 740bhp/380shp
Speed:	13/8kts
Range:	2500nm at 9kts
Armament:	2-18in TT (bow), 2 torpedoes 4-18in torpedoes in external drop-collars (removed) 1-3in AA gun
Complement:	18

2nd Group (*W.3-4*)

As Group 1 except

Dimensions:	149ft 6in (oa) x 17ft x 9ft 6in

19 November 1914 Launch of *W.1* by Armstrong Whitworth on the Tyne.

25 November 1914 *D.2* (Ltd Cdr Head) rammed and sunk by German patrol boat off Borkum, leaving no survivors. Two days earlier her previous CO, Lt Cdr Jameson, had been washed overboard off Harwich.

13 December 1914 *B.11* torpedoed and sunk the old Turkish coast defence ship *Messudieh* in Sari Sighlar Bay, Dardanelles. Her CO, Lt Norman Holbrook, was awarded the Victoria Cross (VC), the first submariner so honoured.

H.23, H.34 and a sister off Portland. (SMM)

Nautilus

*N*autilus was the first named and at the time was the largest submarine built for the Royal Navy. She was designed in response to recommendations for an overseas submarine displacing 1000 tons and capable of 20kts. The provisional order was given to Vickers in 1912 and the keel was laid in March 1913. It took until 1917 to complete the vessel which never became operational. She was renamed *N.1* in 1918.

Nautilus Specifications

Displacement:	1441/2026 tons
Dimensions:	258ft 6in (oa) x 26ft x 17ft 9in
Machinery:	2-shaft diesel, 2 electric motors 3700bhp/1000shp
Speed:	17/10kts
Range:	5300nm at 11kts
Armament:	8-18in TT (2 bow, 4 beam, 2 stern), 16 torpedoes
	1-3in AA gun
Complement:	42

Ten 'F' class were ordered pre-war as successors to the 'E' class, but only three were completed. F.2 is seen here, probably on trials in late 1917. (SMM)

The 'F' Class

T he Admiralty was keen to increase the number of coastal vessels and based the 'F' class on the design of the experimental double-hulled 'V' class with a few minor improvements, the most important being the addition of a stern TT. War service was largely confined to coastal defence.

'F' Class Specifications

Displacement:	353/525 tons
Dimensions:	151ft (oa) x 16ft 1.25ins x 10ft 7in
Machinery:	2-shaft diesels, 2 electric motors, 900bhp/400shp
Speed:	14.5/8.75kts
Range:	3000nm at 9kts
Armament:	3-18in TT (2 bow, 1 stern), 6 torpedoes
	1-2pdr
Complement:	19

16 December 1914	C.9 (Lt Denny) came under fire from bombarding German battlecruisers while trying to leave Hartlepool harbour.
25 December 1914	E.11 (Lt Cdr Nasmith) rescued seaplane crews while under attack by a Zeppelin after the Cuxhaven Raid. D.6 (Lt Cdr Halahan) later sank the seaplanes to prevent their capture.
31 December 1914	Launch of Nautilus by Vickers at Barrow in Furness.
4/5 January 1915	C.31 lost with all hands off Zeebrugge, after being damaged by shore batteries or possibly mined.
18 January 1915	E.10 lost with all hands in Heligoland Bight, probably mined.
31 March 1915	F.1 launched by Chatham Dockyard. The double-hulled coastal boats F.1-3 built 1914-16, five more cancelled.

Lieutenant Maurice Nasmith and his officers and ratings pose for a portrait on the casing of E.11 at Mudros, after forcing the Narrows. (SMM)

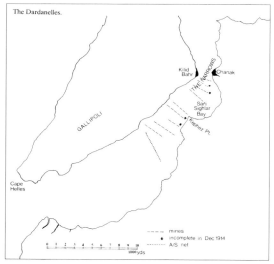

The Dardanelles, showing the Gallipoli peninsula and the dangerous narrows. (CPL)

Turkish prisoners huddle on the casing of E.11 *in the Sea of Marmora.* (SMM)

17 April 1915 *E.15* ran aground off Kephez Point while trying to penetrate the Narrows in the Dardanelles. Her CO, Lt Cdr T Brodie, was killed by gunfire, but the rest of the crew survived as prisoners. After several attempts the wreck was destroyed by two torpedo-armed picket boats the following night.

27 April 1915 *E.14* (Lt Cdr E C Boyle) sailed from Mudros for 21-day patrol in the Sea of Marmora, attacking three targets. Boyle was awarded the VC for his exploits.

30 April 1915 RAN's *AE.2* (Lt Cdr Stoker) sunk by gunfire of Turkish torpedo boat *Sultan Hissar* after five-day patrol in Sea of Marmora. Wreck discovered in 1996 by Turkish divers.

19 May 1915 *E.11* left Kephalo Bay for a 20-day patrol in the Sea of Marmora, during which she attacked five ships. On this patrol her periscope was hit by a lucky shot from a Turkish torpedo boat, and she torpedoed a transport in Istanbul harbour. Like Boyle, Nasmith was immediately awarded the VC.

25 May 1915 *E.11* entered Constantinople harbour, torpedoed a transport and photographed the Golden Horn through the periscope, the first example of periscope photography.

10 June 1915 *E.14* (still commanded by Boyle) began a second patrol in the Sea of Marmora, lasting 23 days. This time she was armed with a 6pdr (57mm) gun, which was used to good effect against small vessels.

21 June 1915 *S.1* (Lt Cdr Kellett) suffered an electrical motor breakdown while submerged off the Horns Reef lightship, but could not surface because a Zeppelin was in the vicinity. Next morning she surfaced close to the German trawler *Ost* and captured her. The *Ost* then set off for Harwich with her captor in tow, but her antiquated steam engine broke down as well. *S.1*'s artificers got it working again, but next day it broke down once more, requiring more assistance. Not until 27 June did *S.1* finally arrive at Harwich in tow of her prize.

While operating with the armed trawler *Taranaki*, *C.2* torpedoed and sank *U.40* off Aberdeen.

24 June 1915 *D.4* sank the grounded German netlayer *Bielefeld* in the Heligoland Bight.

30 June 1915 *E.7* (Lt Cdr A Cochrane) began a 24-day patrol in the Sea of Marmora. Despite his First Lieutenant, Lt Hallifax, and a seaman receiving serious burns, and an outbreak of dysentery, Cochrane succeeded in sinking 13 ships and damaging many more (according to Turkish records).

20 July 1915 While operating with the armed trawler *Princess Louise*, *C.27* torpedoed and sank *U.23* off Fair Isle.

Despite their age, the 'B' class were still operational in 1914, and B.6-11 were ordered from Malta to the Adriatic in 1915 to assist the Italian Navy. B.8 and three sisters are seen here at the Arsenal in Venice, where they were later converted to surface patrol vessels. (SMM)

B.10 loading an 18in torpedo, probably at Venice in 1915. When spares ran out they were converted to surface craft, and were given a raised forecastle and a 12pdr gun, but there is no known photograph of them in their new guise. (SMM)

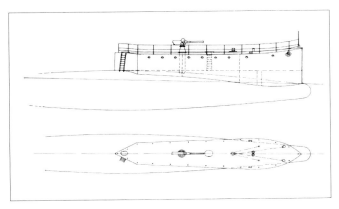

The bow arrangement of B-class as converted for a surface patrol role.
(CPL)

E.11's periscope, hit by a fluke shot from a Turkish torpedo boat in the Sea of Marmora in 1915. (SMM)

4 August 1915 While operating with the armed trawler *Malta*, *C.33* lost with all hands, presumably mined.

8 August 1915 *E.11* torpedoed and sank battleship *Haireddin Barbarossa* in Sea of Marmora.

13 August 1915 *B.6* and *B.11* arrived at Alexandria from Mudros, to prevent Turkish supplies from reaching the Senussi in Libya. Three nights later the two boats were attacked by the Senussi off Sollum and suffered several casualties.

14 August 1915 *E.13* (Layton) and *E.8* (Goodhart) sailed from Harwich on a third attempt to force the Baltic defences. *E.13* ran aground on Saltholm in Danish waters on 17 August, but two days later was wrecked by gunfire of German destroyers, killing 15 of her complement. The wreck was bought by the Danes and scrapped subsequently. *E.8* succeeded, and was later joined by *E.18* (Halahan) and *E.19* (Cromie).

20 August 1915 *E.11*'s first lieutenant, Lt d'Oyly Hughes, swam ashore and blew up railway culvert in the Gulf of Ismid.

29 August 1915 While operating with the armed trawler *Ariadne*, *C.29* was lost with all hands in a German minefield. The wreck was discovered in August 1996, 70 miles NW of Scarborough.

Trawler/submarine Decoy Operations in 1915-16

At least ten 'C' class boats were used as decoys in an effort to trap German U-boats shelling the North Sea fishing fleet. Requisitioned naval trawlers were fitted to tow submerged 'C' class boats, linked by a telephone line. If everything worked the trawler sent details on the U-boat's range and bearing to the submarine, slipped the tow and allowed her to torpedo the U-boat. After a gap the scheme was started again in 1916, but by then the danger from mines was much greater, and it proved far less successful. The submarines known to have been used were:

C.23 - towed by HMT *Ratapiko*
C.24 - towed by HMT *Taranaki*
C.26 - towed by HMT *Wolsey*
C.27 - towed by HMT *Princess Louise*
C.29 - towed by HMT *Ariadne*
C.33 - towed by HMT *Malta*
C.14, C.16, C.21 and C.34 - trawler not identified

E.20 *on completion at Barrow in 1915. Some wartime 'Es' had the more rakish 'cleaver' bow. Launched in June 1915, she was sunk only five months later.* (SMM)

5 September 1915   *E.7* caught in nets off Nagara Point in Dardanelles, and then sunk by primitive form of depth-charge.

15 September 1915   German U-boat *U.6* sunk off Norway by *E.16*.

23 October 1915   *E.8* (Lt Cdr Goodhart) torpedoed and sank the German armoured cruiser *Prince Adalbert* off Libau in Baltic.

6 November 1915   *E.20* (Lt Cdr Warren) torpedoed by German U-boat *UB.14* in Sea

of Marmora. She had been meant to rendezvous with the French *Turquoise*, but the latter had already been sunk and her confidential papers had fallen into Turkish hands.

Launch of *J.1* and *J.2* at Portsmouth Dockyard.

7 November 1915   German light cruiser *Undine* sunk in Baltic by *E.19*.

16 November 1915   *E.11* sank Turkish torpedo boat *Yar Hissar* and a steamer.

14 December 1915   *E.21* (Lt Cdr Harbottle) arrives in Brindisi, the first modern Royal Navy submarine to serve in the Adriatic. As more arrived, the six 'B' class were sent to Venice to work with the Italians.

26 December 1915   *E.6* (Lt Cdr Foster) sunk with all hands by mine near Sunk Light Vessel.

31 December 1915   *E.2* bombarded railway sheds at Mudania, setting them on fire.

6 January 1916   *E.17* (Lt Cdr Moncreiffe) wrecked on sandbank off Texel; crew interned in Holland.

19 January 1916   *H.6* (Lt Stopford) ran aground off West Frisian Islands; crew rescued and interned in Holland. A month later, after she was salved, sold to the Royal Netherlands Navy and became *O.8*.

2 February 1916   *E.2* left the Sea of Marmora, bringing to end the British submarine offensive in the Dardanelles theatre.

18 March 1916   *Swordfish* launched by Scotts at Greenock, the first steam-driven boat in the Royal Navy.

E.20, with her unique 6in howitzer clearly visible, leaves Mudros in October 1915 to make the hazardous passage of the Dardanelles. Days later she was sunk by UB.14 *in the Sea of Marmora, as a result of a major lapse in security by the CO of the French submarine* Turquoise. *(SMM)*

61

The 'J' class were impressive boats. J.4 has a 4in gun in a revolving shield forward of the bridge; this may be a trials view in 1916. The funnel aft does not indicate steam power! It may be a diesel exhaust rigged for surface-running. (SMM)

The 'J' Class

These vessels were a new design of fleet submarine with a high surface speed to counter the (incorrect) intelligence reports of 22kt U-boats. *J.1-8* were ordered in 1915, but original *J.3-4* were cancelled and replaced by renumbered *J.7-8*. Seven 'J' class were built at Portsmouth, Pembroke and Devonport in 1915-16.

'J' Class Specifications

1st Group (*J.1-6*)

Displacement:	1210/1760 tons
Dimensions:	275ft (oa) x 23ft 6in x 14ft
Machinery:	3-shaft diesels, 3 electric motors 3600bhp/1400shp
Speed:	19/9.5kts
Range:	5000nm at 12.5kts
Armament:	6-18in TT (4 bow, 2 beam), 12 torpedoes 1-4in gun
Complement:	44

2nd Group (*J.7*)
As Group 1 except

Displacement:	1260/1820 tons

The rusting remains of HMAS J.7 in Port Phillip Bay, Melbourne. She and her sister were scuttled as breakwaters after being paid off. (SMM)

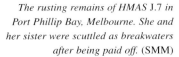

HM Submarine *Swordfish*

Built following the disappointing performance of *Nautilus*, it was hoped that *Swordfish* would be able to reach 20kts. Utilising the steam turbine rejected from the *Nautilus* design, she was built in 1913-16 but never became operational, and was converted to the surface patrol vessel *S.1* in June-August 1917.

Swordfish Specifications

Displacement:	932/1470 tons
Dimensions:	231ft 6in (oa) x 23ft x 14ft 6in
Machinery:	2-shaft steam turbine, 2 electric motors, 3750shp/1400shp
Speed:	18/10kts
Range:	3000nm at 8.5kts
Armament:	2-21in TT (bow), 2 torpedoes, 4-18in TT (beam), 8 torpedoes 2-3in AA guns
Complement:	c18

24 March 1916   *E.24* (Lt Cdr Naper) lost with all hands while laying mines in Heligoland Bight, either by a German mine or a premature explosion of one of her own.

25 April 1916   *E.22* (Lt Cdr Dimsdale) sunk with only two survivors by German U-boat *UB.18* in the North Sea. She had been fitted with a platform on the after casing to launch two Sopwith Schneider floatplanes against Zeppelins.

24 May 1916   *E.18* lost with all hands in Baltic (probably mined).

31 May 1916   Launch of *K.6* and *K.7* at Devonport Dockyard, the first operational steam-driven submarines in the RN. *K.1-17* built 1915-17, to be followed by six of an improved design, *K.23-28* ordered in 1918, of which only *K.26* was completed in 1923.

The ex-cruiser depot ship HMS Arrogant *at Dover in 1916, with G.5 alongside and what appears to be one of the 'W' class.* (SMM)

The Notorious 'K' class

Proposals for a fleet submarine, to be driven by geared steam turbines and a diesel engine on the centre shaft, were made by Vickers to Commodore Hall in April 1915. After discussion a 1913 design was resurrected, and the best features of both were combined in a new design. To save time 18in torpedo-tubes were selected rather than 21in, with beam tubes as in the 'E' class. Two Yarrow boilers in a single stokehold generated steam for a pair of geared steam turbines developing 10,000shp, for a speed of 24kts. An 800hp 'E' class diesel was adopted to drive a 700hp dynamo, the first example of diesel-electric drive in a British submarine.

The armament was heavy, four 18in bow tubes, two 18in beam tubes forward of the boiler room, and a twin pair of revolving tubes in the superstructure. Two 4in guns were also mounted on the forward casing and the superstructure.

Difficulties emerged during trials. They were very complex and marked a big departure from previous standards, so a number of teething troubles arose. The biggest problem was inherent in the concept of the fast submarine; a long, fine-hulled boat could easily plunge below her crush-depth, using the residual steam in the boilers before the electric motors took the load. Contemporary submarines' crush-depths were little more than 50 per cent more than hull-length (they were in effect submersible torpedo boats rather than deep-divers). It was said of the 'Ks' that they handled like destroyers but had the bridge facilities of a picket boat, a picturesque way to describe the risks of mixing submarines with fast-moving surface ships. At night or in bad weather the bridge lookouts in surface ships had difficulty in seeing the low silhouette of a submarine, and the submarine's lookouts were too close to the sea to see much.

Although a spectacular series of collisions and accidents earned the 'K' boats a sinister reputation, they were a major advance in submarine design. It is interesting to speculate what might have happened to the German High Seas Fleet after the Battle of Jutland at the end of May 1916 if it had encountered a flotilla of 'Ks' off the Horns Reef on its way home.

'K' class Specifications

Displacement:	1880/2650 tons
Dimensions:	338ft (oa) x 26ft 6in x 16ft
Propulsion:	2-shaft geared steam turbine, 4 electric motors 10,000shp/1400shp
Speed:	24/9.5kts
Range:	3000nm at 13.5kts
Armament:	10-18in TT (4 bow, 4 beam, revolving twin TT in superstructure) later reduced to 8 TT, 18 torpedoes
	2-4in guns, 1-3in AA gun (1-5.5in gun in *K.17*)
Complement:	59

The steam-driven K.22 *(ex-*K.13*) in her original guise, lowering her funnels before diving. Note that they collapse in opposite directions, and the hatches are already rising to close the apertures. She has the original enclosed wheelhouse and low bridge, but the twin revolving torpedo-tubes are not visible behind their horizontal hatches abaft the conning tower. The guns are a 4in forward and a 3in AA mounting between the funnels.* (SMM)

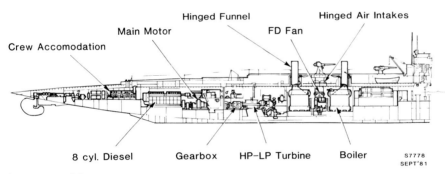

Arrangement of the steam powerplant fitted in K-26. (Institution of Mechanical Engineers)

K.3 in rough weather, probably in 1916 after delivery by Vickers. Note yet another variation in the disposition of armament: a 4in gun ahead of the 3in AA gun on the forward casing, and a second 4in on the casing aft. (BAES Marine)

K.12 differed from her sisters in having the forward 4in gun mounted on a cutwater. She has the graceful 'swan bow' concealing a quick-blowing tank to reduce the risk of diving too deep, and a raised conning tower to allow bridge personnel to see over the bow. (CPL)

K.4 *high and dry, waiting for the tide to refloat her after running aground off Barrow during her trials late in 1916. It was an appropriately inauspicious start to a short career which included two collisions with sister ships, the second of which resulted in her loss during the 'Battle of May Island' in January 1918.*
As with most of the 'K' class, the arrangement of guns seems to be arbitrary, indicating a search for the best solution to reduce spray interference. The 4in gun is on the forward casing, and the 3in AA gun is forward of the forefunnel. Note also the two 18in beam torpedo-tubes and the dark patch hiding the twin revolving tubes in the superstructure.
(BAES Marine)

2 July 1916   *E.26* (Lt Ryan) sunk with all hands off the Ems Estuary, probably by German escorts.

14 July 1916   *H.5* (Lt Varley) sank *U.51* in the Jade River, but incurred Admiralty displeasure because he had ignored orders and left his patrol station 'because he was bored and wished to sink a submarine'. In the next war Varley (no longer in the Navy) was a major protagonist of midget submarines.

15 July 1916   *H.3* (Lt Jenkinson) mined off Cattaro in the Adriatic with no survivors.

August 1916   *C.26, C.27, C.32* and *C.35* left Portsmouth in tow for Archangel, where they were taken on lighters by canal from the White Sea to Kronstadt. As much weight as possible was removed, including batteries.

5 August 1916   *B.10* sunk by Austrian aircraft while lying in the dockyard at Venice, the first Royal Navy submarine to be lost to air attack. Raised two weeks later but accidentally destroyed by fire while under repair.

11 August 1916   *C.33* and her towing trawler *Ratapiko* unsuccessfully attacked an unidentified U-boat.

14 August 1916   Launch of *G.1* at Chatham Dockyard, the first to be armed with 21in torpedoes. *G.1-14* built 1914-17.

Two barges, each carrying a stripped-down 'C' class submarine, en route from Murmansk to the Baltic in 1916 via a network of rivers and canals. Batteries and all movable equipment were removed to lighten the load. (SMM)

The 'G' Class

Built as a response to the latest German designs, the 14 'G' class were constructed with a partial double hull and were armed with a single bow 21in and 4 beam 18in TT. The first vessels had been ordered before the war, while *G.8-13* were ordered in November 1914.

'G' Class Specifications

Displacement:	700/975 tons
Dimensions:	187ft (oa) x 22ft 6in x 13ft
Machinery:	2-shaft diesels, electric motors, 1600bhp/480shp
Speed:	14/10kts
Range:	2400nm at 12.5kts
Armament:	1-21in TT (bow), 2 torpedoes 4-18in TT (beam), 8 torpedoes 1-3in AA gun
Complement:	30

G.4 passing Fort Blockhouse, probably in 1916. She and her sisters were double-hulled boats, the first armed with the 21in torpedo. (SMM)

General arrangement of a G-class. (CPL)

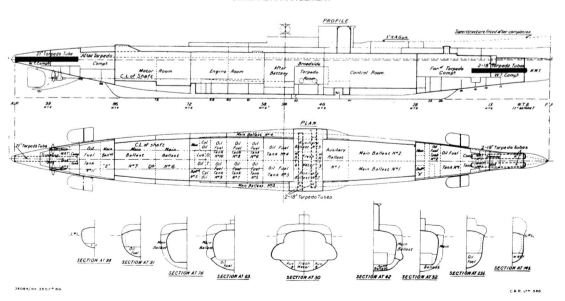

G-CLASS SUBMARINE
GENERAL ARRANGEMENT

An unidentified 'G' class at Barrow in 1916. The boats G.8 to G.13 as well as G.14 (Scotts) and the cancelled G.15 (White), were part of an enormous order placed by Fisher in November 1914 on his return to office as First Sea Lord. (BAES Marine)

15 August 1916   *E.4* (Lt Cdr Tenison) and *E.41* (Lt Winser) collided and sank during a training exercise off Harwich. Only 14 survivors, all from *E.41*, but both boats were raised, repaired and returned to service (*E.41* then became the Royal Navy's first minelaying boat).

21 August 1916   German U-boat *UC.10* sunk off Schouwen Bank by *E.54*.

22 August 1916   *E.16* (Lt Cdr Duff-Dunbar) lost with all hands in North Sea, cause unknown.

22 November 1916   *E.30* (Lt Biggs) lost with all hands in North Sea from unknown cause (probably mined).

30 November 1916   *E.37* (Lt Cdr Chisholm) lost with all hands in North Sea (probably mined).

19 January 1917   *E.36* (Lt MacGregor-Robertson) lost with all hands in North Sea (mined or possibly rammed by *E.43* in night collision).

29 January 1917   *K.13* (Lt Cdr Herbert) sank on trials in Gareloch, with loss of 24 naval personnel and seven civilians. Raised and recommissioned as *K.22* two months later.

10 March 1917   German U-boat *UC.43* sunk off Shetlands by *G.13*.

12 March 1917   *E.49* (Lt Seal) lost with all hands in minefield laid off Shetlands by German U-boat *UC.76*.

17 March 1917   *A.10* sank accidentally at Ardrossan while waiting to recommission (for training only). Raised but not recomissioned.

16 April 1917   While exercising off Harwich with *C.25*, *C.16* (Lt Boase) collided with the escorting destroyer HMS *Melampus* and sank in shallow water with the loss of all hands. She was raised and repaired.

1 May 1917   German U-boat *U.81* sunk off West of Ireland by *E.54*.

10 May 1917   Launch of *L.1* (ex-*E.56*) by Vickers at Barrow in Furness. *L.1-8* built 1916-18.

16 June 1917   *G.9* (Lt Cdr Cary) rammed and sunk in error by destroyer HMS *Pasley* between Lerwick and Norway (only one survivor). She had fired a torpedo at the *Pasley* in error, but it failed to explode, and the destroyer immediately counter-attacked.

E.55, one of the last two 'Es' built, leaving Denny's yard at Dumbarton in 1916. She has all the minor wartime improvements. (SMM)

The 'L' Class

The eight vessels of the 'L' class were ordered in 1916 to replace the rapidly ageing 'E' class. The problems experienced in the double hull experiments forced a return to the tried and tested saddle tank design.

'L' Class Specifications

1st Group (*L.1-8*)

Displacement:	890/1070 tons
Dimensions:	231ft (oa) x 23ft 6in x 14ft
Machinery:	2-shaft diesels, 2 electric motors 2400bhp/1600shp
Speed:	17.5/10.5kts
Range:	3800nm at 10kts
Armament:	4-21in TT (bow), 1-4in gun
Complement:	35

2nd Group (*L.9-33*)

Displacement:	890/1080 tons
Dimensions:	238ft 6in x 23ft 6in x 14ft
Machinery/speed/range:	as Group 1
Armament:	6-21in TT, 1-4in gun 4-21in TT, 1-4in gun, 14 mines (minelayers, *L.11-12, L.14, L.17, L.25*)
Complement:	38

3rd Group (*L.50-74*)

Displacement:	960/1150 tons
Dimensions:	235ft (oa) x 23ft 6in x 13ft
Machinery:	as Groups 1 and 2
Speed:	17/10.5kts
Range:	4500nm at 8kts
Armament:	6-21in TT (bow), 12 torpedoes 2-4in guns
Complement:	44

L.33 in peacetime, possibly on the China Station, showing the characteristic high conning tower and revolving gunshield of the 'L' class. She was the last of the second group, and was paid off in 1931. (SMM)

3 July 1917	*H.13*, *H.16*, *H.17*, *H.18*, *H.19* and *H.20* transferred to Chile as compensation for ships taken over after the outbreak of war.
7 July 1917	German U-boat *U.99* sunk in North Sea by *J.13*.
9 July 1917	Launch of *M.1* by Vickers at Barrow in Furness, the world's first 12in gunned submarine.
17 July 1917	*C.34* (Lt Jefferson) sunk by German U-boat *U.52* while lying on surface near Fair Isle (only one survivor).
20 August 1917	*E.34* (Lt Carre) lost in North Sea from unknown cause (probably mine).
12 September 1917	German U-boat *U.45* sunk off Northern Ireland by *D.7*.
20 October 1917	Launch of *H.21* by Vickers at Barrow in Furness. *H.21-34* and *H.41-52* built 1915-19.
22 October 1917	*C.32* scuttled 22 October 1917 in Gulf of Riga.
1 November 1917	German U-boat *UC.63* sunk in Dover Straits by *E.52*.
3 November 1917	German U-boat *UC.65* sunk in Dover Straits by *C.15*.

E.32 *heading for the open sea, late 1916 or early 1917. Note W/T masts rigged and metal screen on the bridge replacing the inadequate canvas dodger of the early 'Es'.* (Author's collection)

The 'M' Class

M.1-4 were ordered 1916 in place of projected *K.18-21*, but only three were actually completed. The design for a monitor submarine armed with a 12in gun had been suggested by Commodore Hall. Fifty 12in shells could be carried, supplementing the firepower of an attack with the 8-18in torpedoes. Trials with the 12in gun were successful and it was hoped that the vessels would prove their worth in shore bombardments. *M.1* saw brief war service in October 1918 but by then there was no role for a submarine monitor.

Following the loss of *M.1* in 1925, *M.2* and *M.3* were taken in hand for major alterations, *M.2* becoming a seaplane carrier and *M.3* becoming a minelayer. *M.2* was given a large hangar and aircraft handling crane before the conning tower, and a specially designed Parnall Peto floatplane. *M.3* was given a long high casing abaft the conning tower, housing mine rails and winch gear.

M.2 was lost when the hangar door collapsed. Her wreck still lies off Portland and as an official grave for her crew is barred to civilian divers. *M.3* proved very successful, and provided valuable experience for the next generation of dedicated minelayers. The long free-flooding casing was also useful as a promenade for the CO's piper, making her the only one of HM Submarines to be regularly piped in and out of harbour.

'M' class Specifications

Displacement:	1600/1950 tons
Dimensions:	296ft (M.3 303ft) (oa) x 24ft 6in x 16ft
Machinery:	2-shaft diesels, 2 electric motors, 2400bhp/1600shp
Speed:	15.5/9.5kts
Range:	3840nm at 10kts
Armament:	4-18in (M.3 4-21in) TT (bow), 8 torpedoes 1-12in gun, 1-3in AA gun
Complement:	65

M.1 *was the only one of her class to see service at the end of the First World War. The camouflage scheme is experimental, the only known example, but the lack of panchromatic film makes it impossible to guess at the colours.* (SMM)

M.3 *(left)* and M.1 *alongside, with a battleship astern.* (SMM)

In 1927 M.3 was altered to a large minelayer, with the 12in gun removed and a long free-flooding casing added, to protect the twin mine-rails discharging over the stern. She is seen here entering Plymouth. (SMM)

A famous view of M.2 after her conversion to a seaplane carrier, with the Parnall Peto floatplane getting airborne off the short catapult. A number of navies carried out similar experiments in the hope that the floatplane could reconnoitre for targets in distant oceans. (SMM)

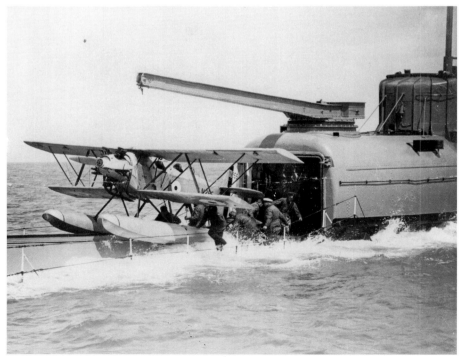

A closer view of M.2's Peto floatplane being readied for takeoff. Note the large crane for hoisting the floatplane into position, and the open hangar door, the ultimate cause of her loss. (SMM)

The 'Battle of May Island'

This disaster was not an actual battle, but it might have been, considering that two submarines were sunk and a light cruiser and a number of submarines were damaged during a sortie by the Grand Fleet on the night of 31 January 1918. Nine 'K' class put to sea with units of the Grand Fleet in the Firth of Forth, but it must be emphasised that the disaster which ensued was not caused by the 'K' design, but it demonstrated the dangers of operating submarines in close proximity to fast-moving surface ships.

Two flotillas of five 'K' class each were involved, the 12th and 13th. A sudden jam of *K.14*'s helm was the trigger, for *K.22* suddenly appeared out of the darkness and rammed her. Minutes later *K.22* was struck a glancing blow by the battlecruiser *Inflexible*. The flotilla leader, the light cruiser *Fearless*, had turned back to find out what had happened to her group of four boats, and she rammed and sank the crippled *K.14*. In the confusion which followed, *K.4* was rammed by *K.6* and *K.17*. Over 100 lives were lost.

The problem for submarines in general is that they have low silhouettes, making them hard for surface ships' lookouts to spot them, and because their bridges are low down, their own lookouts have a limited view. The Court of Enquiry was critical of some of the 'Ks' officers, but as one of participants remarked, they had 'the speed of a destroyer, the turning circle of a battleship, and the bridge control facilities of a picket boat'.

18 November 1917 *K.1* (Lt Cdr Benning) severely damaged in collision with *K.4* off Danish coast. Wrecked sunk by gunfire of HMS *Blanche* after the rescue of the entire crew.

14 January 1918 *G.8* (Lt Tryon) lost in North Sea from unknown cause.

24 January 1918 Launch of *L.10* by Denny Bros. of Dumbarton, first of a new design, the first with a bow salvo of six 21in torpedo-tubes. *L.9-12*, *L.14-27* and *L.33* built 1916-19 (*L.28-32*, *L.36-49* cancelled 1919).

28 January 1918 *E.14* (Lt Cdr G White) sunk by mine off Chanak after abortive attempt to torpedo the stranded German battlecruiser *Goeben*. White was posthumously awarded the VC.

31 January 1918 'Battle of May Island' in Firth of Forth, a catastrophic series of accidents during a night exercise, in which *K.22* rammed *K.14*, was then damaged by a battlecruiser, the light cruiser HMS *Fearless* rammed and sank *K.17*, and *K.4* was rammed and sunk by *K.6*.

1 February 1918 *E.50* (Lt Snook) sunk by mine in North Sea, with all hands.

2 March 1918 *H.5* (Lt Forbes) rammed and sunk in error in the Irish Sea by SS *Rutherglen* (no survivors).

12 March 1918 *D.3* (Lt Maitland-Dougall RCN) bombed and sunk off Fécamp in error by French airship *AT-0*.

3 April 1918 Orders given to scuttle all surviving Royal Navy submarines of Baltic Flotilla off Helsingfors to avoid capture by advancing German troops: *E.1* and *E.19* sunk that day, followed by *C.26*,

A mine and its sinker being loaded aboard E.46 *at Brindisi, probably in 1917.* (SMM)

The minelayer E.46 *at Malta in 1918. The eight port mine chutes can be seen on the saddle tank.* (SMM)

C.27, C.35 and the damaged *E.8* next day.

23 April 1918   *C.3* (Lt Sandford) rammed and destroyed the viaduct linking the Zeebrugge Mole to the shore, preventing the Germans from reinforcing the Mole garrison during the assault and blocking of the Bruges Canal. She and *C.1* (kept back as a reserve) had been packed with explosives and fitted with self-steering gear. All six crew escaped and Sandford was awarded the VC.

25 April 1918   Launch of *R.1* and *R.2* at Chatham Dockyard.

10 May 1918   German U-boat *UB.16* sunk in North Sea by *E.34*, the first half of a remarkable 'double' (see next entry).

11 May 1918   German U-boat *U.154* sunk off Cape St Vincent by *E.35*.

R.4, one of the world's first hunter-killer SSKs, probably post-war. She and R.10 *were retained to work with the anti-submarine training squadron at Portland, where their speed and manoeuvrability made life hard for the trawlers.* (SMM)

The 'R' Class

The 'R' class were the first 'hunter-killer' boats in the world, designed with high underwater speed to hunt U-boats. The machinery arrangement caused surface manoeuvrability problems but the large rudder and fine hull form provided good underwater performance. *R.1-4, R.7-12* were built in 1918 (*R.5-6* cancelled 1919).

'R' Class Specifications

Displacement:	420/500 tons
Dimensions:	163ft (oa) x 16ft x 11ft 6in
Machinery:	2-shaft diesels, electric motors 240bhp/1200shp
Speed:	9.5/15kts
Range:	2000nm at 8kts
Armament:	6-18in TT (bow), 12 torpedoes
Complement:	22

Three 'R' Class, R.12 (outer), R.11 (middle) and either R.7 or R.8, possibly at Killybegs in Donegal or at Blyth, in 1918. (SMM)

12 May 1918   German U-boat *UB.72* sunk in West Channel by *D.6* (Lt Barry). Barry was awarded the DSO.

25 May 1918   German U-boat *UB.52* sunk in Gulf of Genoa by *H.4*.

28 June 1918   *D.6* (Lt Brooks) sunk with all hands by German U-boat *UB.73* off Irish coast.

6 July 1918   *C.25* (Lt Bell) attacked by five German seaplanes while patrolling of Harwich. She suffered heavy casualties, including

A remarkable picture of HM Submarine C.25 under attack from five German seaplanes on 6 July 1918. The bombs bursting around her have killed and wounded crew on the conning tower, and machine gun bullets have pierced her thin pressure hull. She survived but was not repaired. (SMM)

her CO, and was only saved by *E.51*, which arrived and drove off the seaplanes with her deck gun. Not recommissioned.

20 July 1918   *E.34* (Lt Pulleyne) lost by unknown cause in North Sea, no survivors. Her CO had been the only survivor when *B.2* was lost in 1912.

3 October 1918   *L.10* (Lt Cdr A. E. Whitehouse) destroyed by gunfire while attacking damaged German torpedo boat *S.33* off Texel. No survivors, but post-war the dependants were awarded the prize bounty as the torpedo boat was so badly damaged that she had to be sunk by her own side.

15 October 1918   *J.6* (Lt Cdr Warburton) attacked in error by Q-ship *Cymric* off Blyth, and sunk by gunfire with only 15 survivors. An unusual case of double mistaken identity, for *Cymric* mistook *J.6* for *U.6*,

HMCS CH.14 and CH.15 dressed overall, probably to celebrate their arrival in 1920. They spent little more than two years in commission before being paid off for lack of funds, and were scrapped in 1925. (SMM)

and the submarine misidentified the topsail schooner as a German decoy vessel.

16 October 1918 German U-boat *UB.90* sunk in North Sea by *L.12*.

23 October 1918 German U-boat *U.78* sunk in North Sea by *G.2*.

October 1918 *C.12* (Lt Manley) sank accidentally at Immingham when her main motors failed. She was carried by the tide against a destroyer moored alongside a jetty, was holed and sank. Raised but almost certainly not recommissioned (exact date of loss not known).

18 December 1918 Launch of *L.52* by Armstrong Whitworth on Tyne, the last class to be ordered in the First World War. *L.52-56*, *L.69* and *L.71* built 1918-19 (*L.50-52*, *L.57-68*, *L.70* and *L.72-74* cancelled).

A 1918 view of three wartime designs, the minelayer L.12 (left), H.28 (centre) and R.7 (outer). They are possibly serving with the 14th Submarine Flotilla at Blyth. (BAES Marine)

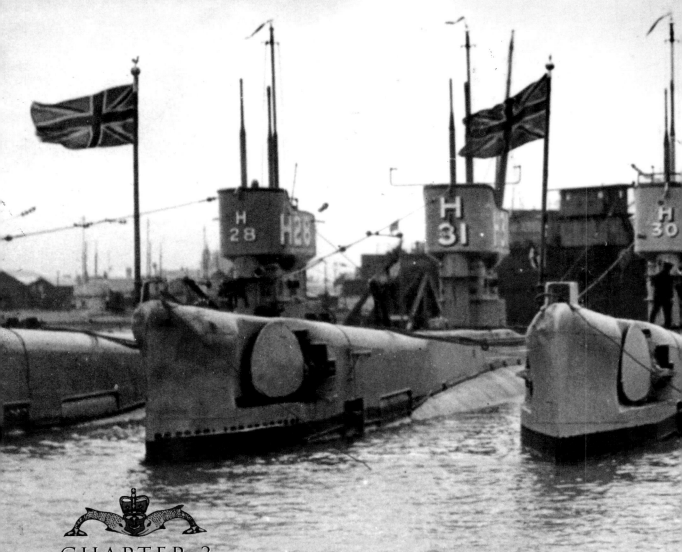

CHAPTER 3
THE INTER WAR

YEARS 1919-1939

FOR THE ROYAL NAVY the Armistice of November 1918 brought no respite, and by the end of the year a start had been made on covering the withdrawal of large quantities of war materiel at Archangel in North Russia. As a classic example of 'mission creep', this limited objective grew into a misguided attempt to contain the Bolshevik Revolution by supporting the counter-revolutionary 'White' forces.

The subsequent British campaigns in the Baltic, the White Sea and the Black Sea resulted in losses, including a light cruiser, a submarine, destroyers, sloops and minesweepers. It also put personnel under great stress; the war was unpopular at home, fostering the feeling of being forgotten, the conditions were often miserable, and Communist propaganda harped on the theme of international capitalism conspiring against the people's revolution. Nor did the 'Whites' inspire any confidence, being undisciplined and brutal. With great relief the British forces turned their backs on the 'Intervention War' in 1920.

The Royal Navy was vastly oversize after the Armistice, and drastic pruning was necessary to get it down to an affordable peacetime level. The submarine service was no exception, and between 1919 and 1923 a melancholy procession of obsolete and relatively new boats were sold for scrapping:

10 'A' class	*Nautilus*
10 'B' class	4 'V' class
27 'C' class	9 'G' class
3 'D' class	8 'H' class
28 'E' class	4 'K' class
3 'F' class	8 'R' class

One 'E' and one 'G' survived until 1928, presumably retained for experimental work. In addition the surrendered *U.126* briefly wore the White Ensign for a period of evaluation. The post-war organisation allowed for 25 of the later 'H' class, 9 'K' class (including the improved *K.26*, completed post-war), three 'M' class, 32 'L' class and two 'R' class for anti-submarine training at Portland. In 1921 serious thought was given for the first time to the future development of the submarine arm. Plans Division identified six types of vessel: fleet, overseas patrol and reconnaissance, cruiser, local defence, mining and anti-submarine. The main consideration was whether the fleet type should be continued.

The brief post-war economic boom rapidly gave way to a slump, and in a misguided attempt to deflate the economy the government returned to the 'gold standard' in 1925 making matters worse. The public was told by its leaders that the recent conflict had been the 'War to end all Wars', and the nation's future lay, not in 'bloated armaments' but in collective security under the benign rule of the League of Nations, established in the Versailles Treaty of 1919. Although the British armed forces needed to retrench, the Treasury made matters much worse in 1919 by imposing a 'Ten Year Rule', stipulating that if the Foreign Office could predict no prospect of a major conflict for ten years, no significant new construction or increase in strength would be funded until the end of that ten-year period. As a short-term measure it might have ensured a useful 'holiday' in major defence expenditure, but the Treasury then insisted on renewing it each year, pushing any major modernisation further and further away. This hit the Navy particularly hard, with its need for major capital expenditure over several years. Submarines came off worst, because only two yards, Vickers and Chatham Dockyard, were equipped for submarine construction, and even when the Ten Year Rule was scrapped in 1933, expanding the submarine-construction capacity proved very difficult.

Previous pages:
Five 'H' class: (left to right) H.28, H.31, H.30, H.23 *and* H.27, *at Fort Blockhouse some time before 1935.*
(BAES Marine)

The Washington Naval Disarmament Conference, convened by the US Government in 1921, marked a serious attempt to head off a new naval arms race. A somewhat half-hearted attempt by the British delegates to abolish the submarine was voted down by the others, who could hardly fail to remember the effectiveness of the U-boats in hamstringing the Royal Navy's undisputed mastery of the oceans in 1914-18. To everyone else, the British attitude was hypocritical, for they above all, owning the world's biggest merchant fleet, were the most vulnerable to submarine attacks. The British, however, had no real hope of achieving abolition, and merely wanted to limit the effectiveness of unrestricted submarine warfare against seaborne commerce. Accordingly the treaty signed in 1922 placed no limit on submarine numbers, although the maximum gun-calibre was fixed at 8in (203mm).

Within a month of voting for abolition, the Royal Navy laid down the giant cruiser submarine *X.1*. She was promoted as an anti-warship submarine, specifically against anti-submarine forces attacking forward-deployed submarines, although perfectly suited to use against merchant ships. With the elimination of the German threat only Japan and the United States seemed to pose a threat in the post war strategic situation. Italy was regarded as friendly, and although the French submarine force was large, a war with France was not viewed as a serious risk. However France had refused to ratify any restrictions on submarine warfare against merchant ships, as proposed by the US Senator Elihu Root.

In May 1922 Admiral Alfred Chatfield, the Assistant Chief of Naval Staff, held a key meeting to decide future Royal Navy submarine policy. Top priority was to be given to overseas patrol types, about a third larger than the latest *L.50* class, habitable in the tropics and having a range of 10,000 miles at economical speed. At American insistence the Anglo-Japanese Treaty had not been renewed, Japan now had to be regarded as a potential enemy and a dozen 'L' class had already been based in China since 1920. A requirement for four minelayers, four cruiser submarines and seven fleet submarines was proposed, but it was decided not to build more cruiser or fleet-types until *K.26* and *X.1* had been fully evaluated. Nor was there any requirement for coast defence or anti-submarine types.

Working within the financial constraints of the 'Ten Year Rule' the Admiralty did its

K.26 was the only one of six Improved 'Ks' ordered in 1918 to be completed. She has two 4in guns in revolving shields, the second at the after end of the superstructure. She was towed from Barrow to Chatham for completion, and served from 1923 to 1931.
(SMM)

best, building a series of overseas patrol boats in small batches, each class showing slight improvements over the last, to supplement and ultimately replace the workhorse 'L' class. In 1922 the strength stood at 44 boats in commission and 11 in reserve, with an intention to build ten patrol type, two cruisers, two fleet boats and two minelayers. Economic realities soon cut out the specialised types, but the 'O' class prototype was funded in the 1923 Programme.

It was hoped to start three more 'Os' in 1924-25, four in 1925-26 and seven each in the following three years, but Winston Churchill, now the Chancellor of the Exchequer, would not permit such extravagance, and no more submarines were funded in the 1924 and 1925 Programmes. Churchill opposed the Admiralty's alternative proposal, eight boats per year, although he preferred submarines to surface ships because they were cheaper. Finally he bowed to pressure from industrial interests and the Admiralty, and it was agreed to build six boats each year from 1926 onwards. Given the general hostility to anything suggestive of rearmament, this was a substantial programme, reflecting well on the Admiralty.

At the Arms Control Conference in Geneva in 1927 the British delegation continued to seek the abolition of submarines. This was again rejected, but two new categories of submarines were agreed: Class 'A' (1600-2000 tons) and Class 'B' (under 600 tons). A proposal to fix American and British total submarine tonnage to 90,000 tons, and the Japanese to 60,000 tons, was rejected by both Americans and Japanese. But the conference broke down on the subject of cruiser-numbers, so it had no effect on submarine policy.

Surprisingly, there was strong support for a fleet submarine, although steam propulsion was no longer considered. Early in 1928 Rear Admiral (Submarines) told the Senior Officers' War Course that a boat with a maximum speed of 21-22kts (in practice a sea

Judging by the number of spectators, this view of M.1 must be after the Armistice, probably in the spring or summer of 1919. If the venue is Devonport the battleship in the background must be HMS Jupiter, *serving as an accommodation ship.* (BAES Marine)

speed of 18-19kts) would be able to play a useful role in fleet actions. Unlike the steam-driven *K.26*, diesels would give a much higher endurance. The 1928 orders were for overseas patrol types, but a new requirement was framed, for a medium-displacement boat suited to operations in confined waters such as the Baltic. This was the genesis of the 'S' design, which had the added virtue of economy. At the same time work started on the design of a 'G' or 'Geneva' design for a fleet submarine. In 1929 four 'Ss' and two fleet boats were to be laid down, but this was reduced to one fleet boat, *Thames*, and two 'S' class. The London Treaty signed in April 1930 reduced maximum submarine displacement to 2000 tons per vessel and gun-calibre to no more than 5.1in (155mm), although each country was allowed three vessels up to 2800 tons with 6.1in guns. The treaty also fixed the total submarine tonnage for all three major naval powers, Britain, the USA and Japan, at 52,700 tons, these limits would expire on 31 December 1936.

The inter-war years were a great time for treaty-makers as the League of Nations and well-meaning statesmen in the democracies tried to restrain the emerging dictatorships in Europe and Japan. In 1932 the League convened a World Disarmament Conference which achieved even less than its predecessors as Germany, finally admitted to the League of Nations in 1926, withdrew from the conference and actually quit the league the following year. The 1936 London Conference, which was meant to replace the Washington agreement, merely underlined the dangers facing the democracies. The conference took place during a period of increased international tension as, despite the threat of sanctions from the League of Nations, Mussolini's Italian forces invaded Abyssinia. Germany did not attend the London Conference and the Japanese delegates walked out, refusing to accept any limitations. This final disappointment for international diplomacy came less than a year after Hitler's renunciation of the Versailles Treaty in May 1935.

H.51 in 1919 off Southsea. She had a short career, being sold for scrapping in 1924. (Author's collection)

Across Europe rearmament accelerated after 1936 and it became increasingly clear that war was inevitable, the only question being when and where? The German invasion of the Rhineland in March 1936 was followed in November by the Rome-Berlin Axis agreement. In July the savage Spanish Civil War had broken out and in the Far East Japanese forces invaded China. France was in very poor shape, and Britain was hardly better, with their armaments industries neglected and in desperate need of modernisation. In this increasingly unstable international situation the British government relaxed the purse strings and the Royal Navy began a huge shipbuilding programme. Including aircraft carriers, battleships, cruisers, destroyers and submarines the plan was to contain the revitalised German Navy (now known as the *Kriegsmarine*) and to forestall a Japanese attempt to enlarge its empire in South East Asia. To meet these commitments, three types of submarine were put into production, an overseas patrol type (the 'T'), improved versions of the medium-sized 'S' design, and finally, a small coastal type for training (the 'U' class).

The battered L.55 *in dry dock at Kronstadt in 1928, after being sunk by two Soviet destroyers in 1919. Salvaged by the Soviet Navy, she was repaired and recommissioned with the same number, and details were incorporated into the Soviet* Leninets *design.* (SMM)

25 March 1919 HM Submarine *J.1* recommissioned into the Royal Australian Navy, with sisters *J.2*, *J.3*, *J.4*, *J.5* and *J.7*. Paid off 12 July 1922 and sold 26 February 1922. Hulk sunk 26 May 1926.

June 1919 *H.14* and *H.15* transferred to Royal Canadian Navy and renumbered *CH.14* and *CH.15*.

4 June 1919 *L.55* sunk by Soviet destroyers in the Baltic. After being raised

H.23, L.19 *and four more 'Hs' passing through the Kiel Canal on a courtesy visit to the Baltic, some time in the 1920s or early 1930s.* (SMM)

by the Soviets in August 1928 she was re-commissioned in the Soviet Navy, retaining her Royal Navy number.

18 October 1919 *H.41* (Lt Cdr Peploe) holed by propeller of depot ship *Vulcan* at Blyth. Raised 18 October but not returned to service.

20 January 1921 *K.5* (Lt Cdr Gaimes) sunk by accident in Bay of Biscay, with the loss of all hands.

H.31 *off Southsea in 1919. The seaplane flying overhead was a standard 'add-on' by private photographers from pre-war days. She was lost in December 1941 in the Bay of Biscay.* (Author's collection)

X.1 at sea, showing her twin 5.2in gun mountings and high freeboard. She was a success, deep-diving and having an exceptional range on the surface, but her German auxiliary diesels were unreliable. She had the unenviable distinction being the only Royal Navy submarine built after the Armistice not to last until the Second World War. (SMM)

The Giants

Plans to build a cruiser submarine dated back to 1915, when the idea was shelved temporarily. The experimental overseas boat *N.1* suffered wartime delays and was overtaken by new ideas, so she never became operational, but useful knowledge was gained for the future. After the surrender of the German Fleet in 1918 the big 'U-cruiser' *U.126* was recommissioned for trials, and yielded further useful information.

The cruiser submarine was ordered in August 1921 from Chatham Dockyard. *X.1* was the last numbered submarine until numbers were reintroduced for a short time in the Second World War. She had a double hull with high freeboard, surmounted by two twin turrets, one at either end of the superstructure. She dived deeply and safely, and had an unrivalled radius of action. Unfortunately the German auxiliary diesels (removed from *U.126*) were a constant source of trouble, and an unrelated accident in dry dock in 1936 proved the last straw, and she was never recommissioned, the only Royal Navy warship built after the Armistice to be scrapped before the outbreak of the Second World War.

X.1 Specifications

Displacement:	2759/3585 tons
Dimensions:	366ft 6in (oa) x 29ft 9in x 15ft 9in
Machinery:	2 shafts, Admiralty 8-cyl diesels (total 6000bhp); MAN 6-cyl diesels (2600bhp); GEC electric motors
Speed:	19.5/9kts
Range:	10,000nm
Armament:	4-5.2in gun in twin mountings 6-21in TT (bow), 12 Mk IV torpedoes
Complement:	109

Said to be the last straw in a career troubled by mechanical problems, X.1 capsized during docking at Portsmouth Dockyard in 1936. She was taken out of service and scrapped at Pembroke. (SMM)

The 'O' Classes

In 1924 a prototype overseas patrol type was ordered from Chatham Dockyard. Originally to be numbered *O.1*, she came into service as the *Oberon*, marking the end of the numbering system which had been used since 1901, apart from *Nautilus* and *Swordfish*. *Oberon* was saddle tank designed, with a depth-limit of 500ft and a test-depth of 200ft. Designed speeds were 15/9kts, but were never attained. Nearly all her fuel was carried in riveted external tanks, causing leakage until replaced by welded tanks in a later refit. She survived the war and was scrapped in 1945.

Oberon Specifications

Displacement:	1598/1831 tons
Dimensions:	269ft 8in (oa) x 28ft x 15ft 6in (mean)
Machinery:	2-shaft Admiralty diesels, electric motors, 2950bhp/1350shp
Speed:	13.5/7.5kts
Armament:	8-21in TT (6 bow, 2 stern), 16 Mk IV/later Mk VIII torpedoes 1-4in 40 cal Mk IV gun (later replaced by Mk XII)
Complement:	54

AO.1 and *AO.2* were laid down in 1925 for the Royal Australian Navy and renamed *Otway* and *Oxley* when delivered in 1927, as replacements for the 'Js'. They served in 5th Submarine Flotilla, but were transferred to the Royal Navy on April 1931 when the RAN submarine force was abolished as an economy measure. They were a Vickers modification of the *Oberon* design, with an improved hullform for slightly higher speed.

Six *Odin* class were laid down in 1927, incorporating improvements to increase speed and a bow shape reminiscent of the ex-RAN *Otway* class. For the first time since 1918, two were ordered from Beardmore. The designed depth limit was 500ft, with a test depth of 300ft, but after *Otus* dived to 360ft hulls were given some stiffening aft. *Orpheus* differed in having Vulcan clutches. War casualties were heavy, four out of six being lost.

Otway class Specifications

Displacement:	1781/2038 tons
Dimensions:	275ft (oa) x 27ft 7.5in x 15ft 8.5in (mean)
Machinery:	2-shaft Admiralty diesels, electric motors, 4520bhp/1390shp
Speed:	17.5/8kts
Armament:	8-21in TT (6 bow, 2 stern), 14 Mk IV or Mk VIII torpedoes 1-4in 40 cal Mk IV (later replaced by Mk XII)
Complement:	53

HMS Odin, *wearing identification letters at the time of the Sino-Japanese War in 1936. She is not armed with a non-standard gun mounting, the shield and 4in gun are trained aft. (SMM)*

HMS Oberon (ex-O.1) was the prototype for the submarines built to replace obsolete First World War boats. (SMM)

25 June 1921	*K.15* (Cdr Bradshaw) sank in the tidal basin at Portsmouth. Not recommissioned.
23 March 1922	*H.42* sunk in collision with destroyer HMS *Versatile* off Gibraltar.
18 August 1923	*L.9*, one of the reserve squadron at Hong Kong, sank in a typhoon. Raised and repaired for another four years' service.
10 January 1924	*L.24* (Lt Cdr Eddis) sunk in collision with battleship HMS *Resolution* off Portland.
12 November 1925	*M.1* (Lt Cdr Carrie) sunk in collision with SS *Vidar* off Start Point.
9 August 1926	*H.29* (Lt Skyrme) foundered at Devonport; raised and sold for scrapping.
24 September 1926	Launch of *Oberon* at Chatham, the first boat of a new post-war programme.
5 May 1928	Launch of *Odin* at Chatham, first of a class of six.
9 July 1929	*H.47* (Lt Gardner) off St Ives Bay sank after collision with *L.12*, with only three survivors.
22 May 1929	Launch of *Perseus* at Barrow in Furness, first of the six *Parthian* class (a month ahead of the lead-boat at Chatham Dockyard).
14 May 1930	Launch of *Rainbow* at Chatham, first of a planned class of six.
10 April 1931	HMAS *Otway* and HMAS *Oxley* transferred from RAN to Royal Navy, retaining their Australian names.

HMS Pandora, *date unknown, but likely to be taken no later than 1934, probably at Devonport.* (BAES Marine)

The 'P' Class

S ix more boats had been laid down in the 1928 programme for completion in 1930-31. The 'P' class were similar to the *Odins*, but were given a new rounded bow. All had Vulcan clutches and *Parthian* had a new type of high-capacity battery. They were the first to be armed with the new Mk VIII torpedo, which would remain in service for another 50 years. *Perseus* was armed with a 4.7in (120mm) 40 cal Mk X gun until 1933, when it was replaced by a standard 4in Mk IV. By the end of the Second World War the surviving boat *Proteus* carried a 20mm Oerlikon gun on a platform at the after end of the conning tower, and could lay 18 M2 mines through her torpedo tubes.

'P' Class Specifications

Displacement:	1475/ 2040 tons
Dimensions:	290ft (oa) x 29ft 9in x 13ft 9in
Machinery:	2-shaft diesels, electric motors, 6000 bhp/2600 shp
Speed:	17.5/9kts
Armament:	8-21in TT (6 bow, 2 stern), 14 Mk VIII torpedoes 1-4in gun, 2 machine guns
Complement:	53

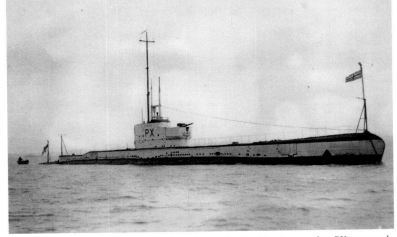

HMS Phoenix *displays a two-tone paint scheme; the identification number PX was used during the Sino-Japanese War in 1936, when it became necessary to reduce the risk from trigger-happy Japanese pilots.* (SMM)

The distinctive ram bow and net cutter of HMS Oxley *and her sister HMS* Otway. *Both were built for the Royal Australian Navy as AO.1 and AO.2, but sold back to the Royal Navy, retaining their Australian names.* (SMM)

HMS Regulus, *one of the last six of the overseas patrol types built since 1925. Note the lower position of the gun mounting and its shield.* (BAES Marine)

The *Rainbow* Class

Six *Rainbow* class were laid down in 1929 to an improved *Parthian* design, with thicker plating (.5inch), welded fuel tanks and a 4.7in gun. *Rainbow* had high-capacity batteries, and by 1945 *Rover* carried a 20mm Oerlikon gun at the after end of the conning tower and could lay 18 M2 mines through her tubes. Two, *Royalist* and *Rupert*, were cancelled as an economy measure in July 1929. These were the last of the cycle which started with the *Oberon* five years earlier. Only *Rover* survived the War.

Rainbow class Specifications

Displacement:	1763/2030 tons
Dimensions:	287ft 2in (oa) x 29ft 11in x 16ft 1in (mean)
Machinery:	2-shaft Admiralty diesels, electric motors, 4640bhp/1670shp
Speed:	17.5/8.5kts
Armament:	8-21in TT (6 bow, 2 stern), 14 Mk VIII torpedoes
	1-4.7in 40 cal Mk IX gun (replaced by 4in 40 cal Mk XII)
Complement:	53

HMS Thames *in Plymouth Sound between 1932 and 1939. Note the weatherproof shield to the 4in gun.* (BAES Marine)

The 'River' Class

Despite its failure in 1916-18, the concept of a fleet submarine was revived in 1930, when plans for a new combined fleet and patrol design were drawn up. It was originally hoped to build 20, but the steady rise of capital ship speeds to 28kts and more finally convinced the Admiralty to cut the programme to three boats, known as the 'River' class.

In fact the prototype *Thames* differed in many details from the later *Severn* and *Clyde*. All had an unusual semi double hull, a 'keyhole' shaped pressure hull and thinner plating to reduce weight; this resulted in a designed diving depth of only 300ft and a test depth of 200ft. External fuel tanks were welded. The design is significant, moreover, in reflecting the advances made in diesel design; a speed of 22kts proved achievable, using turbochargers. These were driven by a pair of 2400bhp auxiliary diesels via generators and motors. Two survived the war.

Thames Specifications

Displacement:	2165/2680 tons
Dimensions:	345ft (oa) x 28ft 3in x 15ft 11in (*Thames* 15ft 7.5in)
Machinery:	2-shaft Admiralty supercharged diesels, electric motors, 10,000bhp/2500shp
Speed:	22.5/10kts
Armament:	6-21in TT (bow), 12 Mk VIII torpedoes 1-4in 40 cal Mk XII gun
Complement:	61

HMS Thames, *first of a new class of fleet submarines, diesel-powered equivalents of the 'K' class intended to work with the battlefleet.* (SMM)

A boatload of survivors from HMS Poseidon, *after she was run down by the Chinese steamer* Yuta *off Weihaiwei in June 1931.* (SMM)

HMS Pandora *pre-war. The torpedo-loading derrick is rigged, suggesting that she may be about to recover a practice torpedo.* (BAES Marine)

9 June 1931   *Poseidon* (Lt Cdr Galpin) rammed and sunk 20nm north of Wei Hai Wei by Chinese steamer *Yuta*. For the first time Davis Escape Apparatus (DEA) was used, allowing several of her crew to reach the surface (22 lost).

8 January 1932   Launch of *Sturgeon* at Chatham, first of a class of four.

26 January 1932   *M.2* (Lt Cdr Leathes) sank off Portland, when the hangar door collapsed and precipitated rapid flooding. All 60 hands, including two RAF personnel, lost.

The 'S' Classes

Another departure was made in 1930, when a new medium displacement saddle tank design was started, for service in restricted waters, particularly the North Sea. Four were laid down in 1930-31, all at Chatham Dockyard, and only one survived the War, operating as the Dutch *Zeehond* from October 1943 to September 1945.

In 1933-36 an improved version, the *Shark* class, was laid down, four at Chatham Dockyard, three at Cammell Laird in Birkenhead, and one at Scotts in Greenock. Design was simplified and improved. Only one survived the War; HMS *Sunfish*, lent to the Soviet Navy as *B.1*, was sunk in error by a British aircraft while en route to Murmansk.

The *Shark* design was adapted for wartime mass-production, with welded framing and a variety of modifications in the light of war experience, such as the addition of radar, a 20mm gun at the after end of the conning tower, and an external torpedo tube aft. In all 50 were laid down in 1940-44 and completed in 1942-45.

'S' class specifications

Displacement:	768/960 tons
Dimensions:	208ft (oa) x 24ft x 11ft 10in (mean)
Machinery:	2-shaft Admiralty diesels, electric motors, 1550bhp/1440shp
Speed:	14/10kts
Armament:	6-21in TT (bow), 12 torpedoes 1-3in gun
Complement:	39

HMS Shark *in late 1939 or early 1940.* (SMM)

THE ROYAL NAVY SUBMARINE SERVICE

The *Porpoise* Class Minelayer

Designed with a saddle-tank hull similar to the 'P' class, this vessel was laid down in 1931 with a completion date of 1933. In 1934 the 4.7in gun was replaced by a 4in Mk XII. Later the 12 torpedoes could be replaced by 12 M2 mines.

Porpoise Specifications

Displacement:	1500/2053 tons *Narwhal* group 1520/2157 tons
Dimensions:	288ft (oa) x 29ft 9in x 13ft 9in *Narwhal* group 289ft x 25ft 6in x 15ft 6in
Machinery:	2-shaft diesels, electric motors, 3300 bhp/1630 shp
Speed:	15/8.75kts
Armament:	6-21in TT (bow), 12 torpedoes 1-4.7in gun 2 .305 cal machine guns 50 mines
Complement:	59

HMS Cachalot, *one of six dedicated minelayers. The high extended casing conceals the mine deck.* (SMM)

A very new Porpoise *class minelayer, still with plating marks, running constructor's sea trials (CSTs) off Barrow in 1935 or 1936. She is either the* Narwhal *or the* Rorqual. *(BAES Marine)*

Four of the Porpoise *class minelayers lying at HMS* Dolphin *in the late 1930s. The second boat from the left is HMS* Porpoise. *The concept of the minelaying submarine was overtaken by the development of the tube-launched mine.* (SMM)

HMS Porpoise *puts to sea, showing the doors to the mine deck and the end of the chain drive for hauling the Mk XVI mines aft. As each mine was laid the boat took on board an equivalent weight of water to maintain trim. This capacious deck was used during the Second World War to run vital stores into Malta such as cased petrol, food, glycol coolant for Spitfire engines, and even baby food, via the 'Porpoise Carrier Service'.* (BAES Marine)

HMS Triad *on trials off Barrow just before the outbreak of war. She belonged to the first group, with forward-firing external torpedo-tubes abreast of the conning tower.* (BAES Marine)

Triton class ('T' Class prewar)

When the plan to build more *Thames* class was dropped, in its place a new patrol design was prepared. It was a saddle tank design, with a heavy bow salvo to improve the likelihood of a hit at long range. Initially two extra external torpedo tubes were positioned in a bulbous bow, and another two flanking the conning tower, making a total of ten. The external bow tubes were removed from some boats, and in all, the midships tubes were reversed and repositioned in the after casing. Later an additional external stern tube was provided. To deal with the air threat (theoretically) and for use against 'soft' targets, a single 20mm Oerlikon gun was added, on a 'bandstand' at the after end of the conning tower, as in other classes. Another group of 16 was laid down in 1939-1942, incorporating welded framing, followed by 22 more in 1941-44.

'T' Class Specifications (as designed)

Displacement:	1290/1560 tons
Dimensions:	276ft 6in (oa) x 25ft 6in x 14ft 7in (max)
Machinery:	2-shaft diesel/electric; 2-2500bhp diesels, 4-1450shp electric motors; 5000bhp/5800shp; 336 battery cells
Speed:	15.5/9kts
Range:	4500nm at 11kts
Armament:	10-21in (533mm) torpedo-tubes (6 internal, four external), 16 Mk VIII torpedoes (or tube-launched mines) 1-4in (102mm) gun
Complement:	48 officers and ratings

Undine class ('U' class prewar)

The age of the 'H' class led to the building of three small boats in 1937-38 by Vickers Armstrong. They were single-hulled and had electric drive, running on the surface with the main motors driven from the diesel-generators. Designed for training and local patrols and initially intended to be unarmed, four torpedo tubes were later added forward, the external two were housed in a bulbous bow. Only *Ursula* carried the 3in gun and as a consequence could only carry 8 torpedoes.

'U' Class Specifications (prewar)

Displacement:	540/730 tons
Dimensions:	191ft 6in (oa) x 16ft x 12ft 9in
Machinery:	2-shaft diesels, electric motors, 615 bhp/825shp
Speed:	11.75/9kts
Armament:	6-21in TT (4 bow internal, 2 external), 10 torpedoes
	1-3in gun
Complement:	27

Launch of Undine *at Barrow in 1937, first of three 'U' class ordered as replacements for the surviving 'H' class. Only she and her sisters* Unity *and* Ursula *had two external torpedo-tubes, housed in the large bulbous bow. (BAES Marine)*

29 January 1932   Launch of *Thames* at Barrow in Furness, first of a class of three.

30 August 1932   Launch of prototype minelayer *Porpoise* at Barrow in Furness.

16 March 1934   Launch of *Sealion* at Birkenhead, first of a class of eight.

29 August 1935   Launch of *Narwhal* at Barrow in Furness, first of a class of five minelayers.

The *Thetis* Accident

The primary cause of the disaster was subsequently found to be a torpedo tube door indicator installed incorrectly. The torpedo officer inadvertently inspected a torpedo tube when the outer door was open. Other contributory causes were the inability of crew-members to shut the forward watertight door, and a series of avoidable delays in getting a rescue operation underway.

In addition to the submariners on board, a number of key members of the builders' design team were lost. As a result wartime submarine building at Cammell Laird's Birkenhead yard experienced many difficulties. As result of this unexpected side-effect, wartime trials of submarines were conducted with only a limited number of shipyard personnel on board. A new design of watertight door clip, known as the *Thetis* clip, permitted much more rapid closing of doors in the event of an accident.

Vain attempts to secure the after end of HMS Thetis, *after it briefly broke surface following her diving accident in Liverpool Bay in June 1939.* (SMM)

5 October 1937   Launch of *Triton* at Barrow in Furness, first of a class of 15.

Launch of *Undine* at Barrow in Furness, first of a class of three.

1 June 1939   *Thetis* (Lt Cdr Bolus) sunk by accident in Liverpool Bay while carrying out diving trials. Raised and repaired, then recommissioned as *Thunderbolt*.

An early 'U' class, probably HMS Undine, *at sea. As completed she and* Unity *had no 3in gun fitted.*
(BAES Maritime)

CHAPTER 4

THE SECOND WORLD WAR
1939-1945

WHEN GREAT BRITAIN AND FRANCE declared war on Germany on 3 September 1939, the Royal Navy and its submarine arm in particular, showed how badly it had been neglected during what Winston Churchill called the 'locust years' of retrenchment and faith in the ability of the League of Nations and collective security to check the rise of Fascism.

The problems facing the Allies were acute. Rearmament had officially started in 1936, but French industry had been dislocated by the reckless policies of the Popular Front, and British industry had been sorely battered by the Great Depression. To get a massive naval building programme under way it was first necessary to rebuild and re-equip shipyards and ordnance factories. Strategically, Germany was less isolated than it had been in 1914, having signed a Non-aggression Pact with the Soviet Union and cultivated the Italian dictator Benito Mussolini.

The German *Blitzkrieg* on Poland in 1939 was followed by successful attacks on Denmark, Norway and France in 1940. With the strategic situation on the continent rapidly degenerating the British Expeditionary Force fell back to Dunkirk where 338,000 troops were evacuated in the 'Nine Days Wonder', 26 May to 3 June 1940. Without French opposition the German armed forces had access to the English Channel and Atlantic coasts. Germany's stunning conquest of Western Europe provided naval bases from Norway down to the Bay of Biscay, and in theory access to the industrial resources of all the occupied countries. In Southern Europe German military success had prompted Italy to abandon neutrality and join the war against the allies on 8 June and Italian forces were soon attacking the south of France. With its armed forces in the north destroyed by the German *Blitzkrieg* and now faced with a war on two fronts on 25 June the French signed an armistice with Germany.

The British strategic position seemed almost hopeless as the French capitulation and Italian entry into the war virtually turned the Mediterranean into an Axis lake. British distrust of Italian intentions led the Cabinet to take drastic action to prevent an Axis *coup de main* against the French fleet, still the fourth largest in the world, and to the melancholy sight of the Royal Navy attacking its former ally at Oran in July 1940. This is not the place to discuss the details of the negotiations, or even the risk of the French ships falling to Italian or German hands, apart from pointing out that neither of the dictators had a reputation for honest dealings. While the swift and brutal action helped to send a message to the United States and any doubters that the British were not about to surrender to Hitler, it created bitter divisions among the French military. Although many officers and ratings declared their willingness to rally to Colonel de Gaulle's French government-in-exile, others refused to cooperate with the British.

Whatever the arguments about Oran, the Germans were quick to exploit their victory on land, and within days the U-boat Arm moved resources to the Atlantic coast of Normandy and Brittany, to establish bases and to adapt existing French dockyards to their own needs. From there the U-boats and surface ships could quickly reach the hunting grounds of the North Atlantic and with greatly reduced risk of interception. Therefore by late 1940 the Axis powers had the bases across Europe close to vital British shipping lanes in home waters and on the routes to the Far East and North America necessary for an effective submarine offensive. The Battle of the Atlantic had started, and would continue with undiminished ferocity until 1945.

Operation 'Barbarossa', Hitler's attack on the Soviet Union in June 1941, brought the industrial might of Russia into the war on the Allied side, but the initial successes of the German armies meant that Hitler added even more territory to the Third Reich. Similarly, the Japanese attacks on Pearl Harbor and Malaya in December 1941 turned a European

Previous pages:
HMS Saracen *running trials in the Irish Sea in 1942.* (SMM)

Three early 'S' class lying alongside their depot ship. (SMM)

war into a world-wide conflict, and brought the United States into the war against Germany and Italy. But it was to be a long, hard road to victory, with many setbacks in 1942-43.

As the war in Europe developed in a struggle for national survival, the British Government was faced with an unpleasant strategic discovery. Britain could fight a war against Germany in Europe or a war against Japan in the Far East, but could not commit enough resources to both theatres at the same time. Promises made to Australia of a 'main fleet' to be sent out to Singapore (described in contemporary newspapers as the Gibraltar of the Far East) could not be honoured. In the event Churchill fell into the trap of underestimating the Japanese, and sent out two capital ships, HMS *Prince of Wales* and HMS *Repulse*, to 'overawe' them. They were sunk on 10 December by Japanese aircraft shortly after the Japanese army invaded northern Malaya. After a relatively short siege on 15 February 1942 the fortress of Singapore fell to a numerically smaller Japanese army. The British Empire had been struck a near-mortal blow.

Any hope that the entry of the United States into the war would suddenly turn the tide against the Axis nations was dashed by the aftermath of Pearl Harbor. The US Navy was on the strategic defensive until the Pacific Fleet could be reinforced with new aircraft carriers and their escorts, and all the while Japanese armies swept through the East Indies until they were within striking distance of Australia. The armed forces of the Japanese Empire seemed invincible, and well into 1942 the Allies seemed to be able to do little more than delay their ultimate victory.

Fortunately for the Allies, they had two hidden advantages over their opponents. The

Rear Admiral Max Horton, Flag Officer Submarines (FOSM) for the first two years of the Second World War. He was the Navy's most successful submariner, having dominated the sea war in the Baltic during 1915-16. At the end of the First World War he commanded M.1. (SMM)

Lieutenant Commander R D Cayley on the bridge of HMS Utmost. *(SMM)*

first was intelligence, as both the Americans and the British had great success in cracking Japanese and German ciphers and codes. The second was a rapidly developing technical and industrial edge, which was to win ultimate victory in the Atlantic and the Pacific. This is not to say that the Germans or Japanese could not come up with innovative and unorthodox technical solutions, but neither nation ever solved the problem of exploiting scientific developments.

The work of codebreakers enabled the Allies to read German operational orders to the U-boats, and provided the US Navy with its great victory at Midway in June 1942. Technology in the form of radar, asdic (now known as sonar) and more powerful weapons ground down the U-boats and enabled the US Navy carriers to destroy the Imperial Japanese Navy's super carrier aircrews. Incidentally, both asdic and radar made submarines much more effective.

Midway marked the turning point in the Pacific, and although the Japanese continued to fight with great courage and aggression, they were henceforward defending a perimeter of island bases. When the American fast carrier task forces breached that perimeter it was only matter of time before the Home Islands came under direct attack. In the Atlantic the turning point came in the spring of 1943. In early March there were 70 U-boats in the Atlantic ready to attack Allied convoys. During the savage convoy battles of that month they sank 627,377 tons of allied shipping forcing the Admiralty to reassess the strategic situation. However, the situation was turned decisively in the Allies favour by the arrival in April of the Very Long Range Liberator which closed the Mid-Atlantic air gap. In late April an epic battle was fought around convoy ONS5. Attacked by 40 U-boats over the course of ten days the convoy escorts managed to drive off the assailants, the use of radar proving essential to the tactical victory. In May alone total U-boat losses reached 41, a shocking figure for the Germans which forced a temporary halt to the strategic offensive. This was not a total collapse of the U-boats offensive but an admission by the U-boat Command that it had been forced on the defensive for the first time in three years. Although a brave effort was made to re-group and re-equip, the U-boats never regained the initiative.

In the Mediterranean the Allies attacked Sicily in July 1943 and by September were in a position to cross the Straits of Messina and assault the Italian mainland. However, just as a secondary landing was about to begin at Salerno, Italy decided to desert its German partners and on 10 September surrendered its fleet to Admiral Andrew Browne Cunningham, Commanded-in-Chief of the Allied naval forces in the Mediterranean. The Germans reacted swiftly, turning on the Italians and coercing many of them into carrying on the war as reluctant allies. The Salerno landings took place as planned, but German forces put up a stubborn resistance inflicting heavy losses on the Allies. With *Valiant* and *Warspite* providing vital naval gunfire support the Allies pushed back the defending forces, gaining a foothold in Southern Italy. An attempt to outflank the Germans by a second amphibious landing at Anzio the following year ran into serious opposition, and became bogged down, but gradually the German defenders were pushed northwards.

On 6 June 1944 operation 'Overlord', the Allied invasion of Western Europe, was launched. The actual assault on the Normandy coastline, codename 'Neptune' was the greatest amphibious landing in history. On D-day itself 6,833 ships landed over 130,000 Allied troops over five beaches. It marked the opening of the Second Front, an offensive in the West to match the steady advance of the Red Army towards Berlin. Although the D-Day landings were not decisive in the strictest sense, they were the first step in the liberation of Western Europe, and gave reality to the German High Command's greatest nightmare, a war on two fronts. By the spring of 1945 the ceaseless bombing of German cities and the crushing of the *Luftwaffe* and *Wehrmacht* brought the Third Reich to its knees, and forced its leaders to accept unconditional surrender.

The Royal Navy's submarines played the same role in the North Sea as they had in 1914-18, reconnaissance and interdiction of naval movements. In September 1939 the Royal Navy entered the war with 58 submarines, still including 11 'H' class and three 'L' class. The rest of the force included:

9 'O' group
6 'P' class
4 'R' class
3 'River' class
12 'S' class
6 *Porpoise* class
4 'T' class (+ 34 building or ordered)

As in 1914-1918 Germany lacked sufficient merchant ships to give an opportunity for a war on seaborne commerce, but Royal Navy submarines inflicted severe losses on the *Kriegsmarine* in the Norwegian campaign. When Italy entered the war in mid-1940 submarines became essential to neutralise the Italian Navy and keep the central

Mediterranean basin open to British ships. In a far-sighted move the strategically vital submarine base at Malta had been provided with bombproof shelters in the sandstone cliffs, allowing the island to play a crucial role. The clear waters of the Mediterranean were, however, very dangerous for submarines, and losses were heavy. The older boats proved particularly vulnerable, whereas the smaller 'Us' and 'Ts' proved more suitable.

When Malta became too dangerous for surface ships essential supplies were brought in by submarine, and during daylight hours the boats based at Malta were forced to rely on smokescreens. When the aerial bombardment became even heavier, they were forced to lie on the bottom of Grand Harbour during daylight, surfacing at night for essential maintenance.

When the time came to reinforce the American offensive against Japan, the smaller British 'S' and 'T' class submarines proved their worth in being able to operate in coastal waters too shallow for the large US Navy boats.

Despite the extravagant pre-war claims that airpower had made armies and navies obsolete, it had turned out to be a naval war again. Both Germany and Japan were defeated by conventional forces which inflicted mounting losses of manpower. As an island empire, Japan could only be attacked by projecting military power across the Pacific, and similarly, American industrial and military power could only be brought to bear on Germany if the Atlantic was controlled by Allied seapower.

HMS Clyde, *one of three 'River' class fleet submarines. It must be early in the Second World War as she is camouflaged. (SMM)*

10 September 1939   *Oxley* (Lt Cdr Bowerman) accidentally torpedoed by HMS *Triton* off Norway. She had apparently strayed out of her patrol area and was mistaken for a U-boat. Only two survivors.

4 December 1939   *U.36* torpedoed by *Salmon* (Cdr Bickford) SW of Stavanger, the first German U-boat sunk by a British submarine.

13 December 1939   *Salmon* (Lt Cdr Bickford) hit the German light cruisers *Leipzig* and *Nürnberg* with a single torpedo each, damaging them

severely. The previous day the 51,000-ton troopship *Bremen* narrowly avoided being sunk by the *Salmon*.

26 December 1939 *Triumph* had her bow blown off by a mine in Norwegian waters but survived.

7 January 1940 *Undine* (Lt Cdr A S Jackson) sunk in Heligoland Bight, depth-charged by German minesweepers.

Seahorse (Lt Dawson) sunk in Heligoland Bight, probably depth-charged by German minesweepers. All hands lost.

9 January 1940 *Starfish* (Lt Turner) depth-charged by German minesweepers in Heligoland Bight, after an unsuccessful attack on a destroyer. All saved.

19 March 1940 *Ursula* (Cdr Phillips) sank MV *Heddernheim* in the Kattegat.

23 March 1940 *Truant* (Lt Cdr Hutchinson) damaged MV *Edmond Hugo Stinnes* in the Kattegat; the victim was later scuttled.

8 April 1940 *Trident* (Lt Cdr Seale) sank the German tanker *Posidonia* off Skagen. Later that day she attacked the heavy cruiser *Lützow*, but without success.

9 April 1940 *Truant* damaged the German light cruiser *Karlsruhe* off Kristiansand. The cruiser was later sunk by German light forces.

10 April 1940 *Thistle* (Lt Cdr Haselfoot) torpedoed by German U-boat *U.4* off Utsira. No survivors.

Spearfish (Lt Cdr Forbes) hit the *Lützow*, causing heavy damage.

Triton sank the merchant ships *Friedenau* and *Wigbert* and escort *R.6*.

11 April 1940 *Triad* sank the merchant ship *Iona*.

12 April 1940 *Salmon* torpedoed German U-boat *U.54* in North Sea.

15 April 1940 *Sterlet* (Lt Cdr Haward) torpedoed German gunnery training ship *Brummer* off Oslofjord, causing her to sink the next day.

18 April 1940 *Sterlet* depth-charged by German minesweepers in Skagerrak, and lost with all hands.

20 April 1940 *Triad* sank unidentified German merchant ship.

Tarpon (Lt Cdr Caldwell) depth-charged by German decoy ship

Lieutenant Commander Edward Bickford at the periscope in the control room of HMS Salmon. *He had a short but successful career, damaging two German light cruisers and sinking a U-boat before being mined off Norway in 1940. (SMM)*

Ratings on board HMS Sealion *tuck into a 'full English' breakfast. The accommodation in the medium-sized 'S's was not as cramped as the 'U' class or their predecessors in the First World War. (SMM)*

Schiff 40 in North Sea. No survivors.

Launch of *Utmost* at Barrow, the first of the 'U' War Emergency and 1940 Programmes and the 1941 'short hull' design.

29 April 1940 *Unity* (Lt Brooks) sunk in collision with Norwegian merchant ship *Atle Jarl* off Blyth. Two lost.

'U' class War Emergency, 1940 Programmes and 1941 'short hull' design

It was soon realised that the cheap and simple design of the *Undine* class would be useful in restricted waters, and an improved design was drawn up for wartime mass-production. In all 49 of these 'short hull' designs were laid down in 1939-43 and completed 1940-43. There were no external TT, instead 6 M2 mines could be carried in place of the 8 torpedoes. The 12pdr was later replaced by a 3in gun.

HMS *Urchin* served as the Polish *Sokol*, *P.47* became the Dutch *Dolfijn* in 1942, *Unbroken* and *Unison* went to Russia as *B.2* and *B.3* in 1944, *Uredd* and *Varne* went to Norway in 1941 and 1943 respectively, *Untiring* and *Upstart* became the Hellenic *Xifias* and *Amfitriti* in 1945, and *Vox* became the French *Curie* in 1943.

'U' class Specifications (improved)

Displacement:	630-646/732 tons
Dimensions:	191ft-196ft 10in (oa) x 16ft 1in x 14ft 10in-15ft 3in (max)
Machinery:	2-shaft Paxman-Ricardo or Paxman diesels, electric motors, 615bhp/825shp
Speed:	11.25/10kts
Armament:	4-21in TT (bow), 8 torpedoes 1-12pdr
Complement:	31-33

HMS Upstart *being formally handed over to the Hellenic Navy in 1945. She was renamed* Xifias *and was returned in 1952.* (SMM)

2 May 1940   *Trident* damaged German merchant ship *Clara Stinnes*.

5 May 1940   *Seal* (Lt Cdr Lonsdale) damaged by mine in Kattegat on 4 May and forced to surrender a day later. Renamed *UB* in German service and used for training; scuttled at Kiel 3 May 1945 but later raised and scrapped.

23 May 1940   *Truant* sank German merchant ship *Preussen*.

13 June 1940   *Odin* (Lt Cdr Woods) sunk by gunfire and depth-charges from the Italian destroyer *Strale* in Gulf of Taranto.

16 June 1940   *Grampus* (Lt Cdr Rowe) depth-charged by Italian torpedo boats *Circe* and *Clio* off Syracuse. No survivors.

Tetrarch sank German tanker *Samland*.

19 June 1940   *Orpheus* (Lt Cdr Wise) depth-charged by Italian destroyer *Turbine* off Tobruk. No survivors.

20 June 1940   *Parthian* torpedoed the Italian submarine *Diamante* off Tobruk.

Clyde (Lt Cdr Ingram) scored a single hit on the German battlecruiser *Gneisenau*, putting her out of action for six months.

5 July 1940   *Shark* (Lt Cdr Buckley) badly damaged by air attack off

HMS Shark *was forced to the surface off southern Norway by damage from German aircraft in July 1940. Seen here from a German ship, her crew are awaiting rescue, but she sank in the Kattegat before the Germans could get her home as a prize.*
(SMM)

Skudesnes. The survivors surrendered but the boat sank in tow SW of Stavanger.

9 July 1940   *Salmon* lost with all hands, probably by mine, off Skudesnes.

16 July 1940   *Phoenix* (Lt Cdr Nowell) depth-charged by Italian torpedo boat *Albatros* off Sicily. No survivors.

23 July 1940   *Narwhal* (Lt Cdr Burch) bombed by German aircraft in North Sea. No survivors.

26 July 1940   *Thames* (Lt Cdr Dunkerley) torpedoed German torpedo boat *Luchs* W of Skagerrak.

1 August 1940   *Oswald* (Lt Fraser) rammed by Italian destroyer *Ugolino Vivaldi* SE of Cape Spartivento. Three of her crew lost.

Spearfish (Lt Cdr Forbes) torpedoed by German U-boat *U.34* WSW of Stavanger. Only one survivor.

2 August 1940   *Thames* lost, probably mined, between Lister and Kristiansand, after attacking the torpedo boat *Luchs*.

20 August 1940   *Cachalot* torpedoed German U-boat *U.51* in Bay of Biscay.

2 September 1940   *Tigris* sank German escort trawler.

22 September 1940   *Truant* sank Italian merchant ship *Provvidenza*.

Osiris torpedoed Italian torpedo boat *Palestro*.

Tuna sank German merchant ship *Tirranna*.

24 September 1940   *Tuna* sank German merchant ship *Ostmark*.

The engineroom of a wartime submarine. The crew are at diving stations, with the diesels stopped and the electric motors about to be clutched in. (Author's collection)

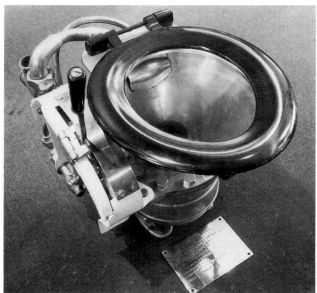

The 'heads' of a 1940-vintage submarine, with a brass plate on the deck listing the eight 'things to do' (in fact 11 separate actions) to avoid 'getting your own back'. (NMM)

Allied Submarines

After the fall of Poland in 1939 and France, the Netherlands and Norway in 1940, governments-in-exile were set up in London. A number of submarines and surface vessels escaped as well, and these became the nucleus of a number of 'Free' navies. Providing spares for foreign-built boats was a headache, and some of the submarines were somewhat elderly, but enthusiasm and patriotism went a long way to offset problems. For example, when the Free French minelayer *Rubis* ran out of Sautter-Harlé mines, Vickers was able manufacture new mines based on a similar type supplied with two Estonian boats pre-war.

As numbers of 'U' and 'V' class boats became available, some were transferred to these Allied forces, and eventually provided some of them with the basis for a post-war force. Greece and Russia were added to the list in 1941, and also received submarines from the Royal Navy. Four boats building for Turkey in 1939 were retained by the navy and the three survivors were returned at the end of the war.

P.614, *formerly the Turkish* Burak Reis, *was one of four taken over by the Royal Navy after the outbreak of war. She was used for training at Freetown, Sierra Leone in 1942, then returned to Home waters for the same duty in 1943. She was returned to Turkey in 1945 under her original name.* (SMM)

4 October 1940   *Triton* sank Italian merchant ship *Fassio*.

15 October 1940   *Triad* (Lt Cdr Salt) lost by unknown cause off Benghazi (possibly mined or bombed by Italian aircraft), off Benghazi. No survivors.

Rainbow (Lt Cdr Moore) lost in close-range gun battle with Italian submarine *Enrico Toti* off Calabria, the only known surface action between two submarines. No survivors.

L.17 hit a 7000 ton merchant ship with three torpedoes off Cherbourg.

18 October 1940   *H.49* (Lt Coltart) depth-charged by German trawlers *Uj.116* and *Uj.118* W of Texel, with only one survivor. Wreck discovered in 1984.

2 November 1940   *Taku* sank German tanker *Gedania*.

7 November 1940   *Swordfish* (Lt Langley) sunk by mine S of St Catherine's Point, Isle of Wight. Wreck located in 1983.

13 November 1940   *Tigris* sank sailing vessel *Edmond*.

'T' class War Emergency and 1940 Programmes

Designed to improve on the prewar *Triton* class, these 16 vessels had welded framing, a 20mm AA gun and 5 external TT. The external tubes underwent successful minelaying trials in *Trusty* in August 1941, following this 18 M2 mines could be carried instead of torpedoes.

'T' class Specifications (improved)

Displacement:	1327/1567-1575 tons
Dimensions:	273ft 3in-275ft (oa) x 26ft 7in x 14ft 7in-14ft 10in (mean)
Machinery:	2-shaft Vickers or Admiralty diesels, electric motors, 2500bhp/1450shp
Speed:	15.25/9kts
Armament:	11-21in TT (6 bow, 5 external) 17 torpedoes
	1-4in 40 cal Mk XII gun, 1-20mm AA gun
Complement:	61

HMS Thorn, *one of the second group of 'Ts', shows her remodelled bow with two external tubes. Its purpose was to reduce the spray thrown up by the original 'T' bow. The torpedo-tubes abreast of the conning tower are repositioned to fire aft. She was built by Cammell Laird at Birkenhead.* (SMM)

27 November 1940 *Talisman* (Lt Cdr Francis) captured fishing vessel *le Clipper* off St Nazaire for use as intelligence-gatherer.

28 November 1940 Launch of *Thrasher* at Birkenhead, first of the 'T' class War Emergency and 1940 programmes.

c6 December 1940 *Regulus* (Lt Cdr Currie) lost from unknown cause, probably mined, in Straits of Otranto.

c7 December 1940 *Triton* (Lt Cdr Watkins) lost. She had probably damaged the Italian liner *Olimpia* on 6 December and was sunk by torpedo boats.

13 December 1940 *Truant* sank Italian merchant ship *Bianchi*.

15 December 1940 *Thunderbolt* (ex-*Thetis*, Lt Crouch) torpedoed Italian submarine *Capitano Tarantini* in Bay of Biscay.

16 December 1940 *Truant* sank Italian tanker *Bonzo*.

18 December 1940 *Tuna* sank unidentified tug.

3 February 1941 *Truant* sank Italian merchant ship *Multedo*.

11 February 1941 *Snapper* (Lt Prowse) depth-charged by German minesweepers SW of Ushant.

12 February 1941 *Tigris* sank unidentified merchant ship.

19 February 1941 *Tigris* sank German merchant ship *Guilvinec*.

25 February 1941 *Upright* torpedoed Italian light cruiser *Armando Diaz*.

5 March 1941 *Triumph* sank Italian merchant ships *Marzamemi* and *Lo Faro* in the Mediterranean.

12 March 1941 *Thunderbolt* torpedoed Italian merchant ship *Esterel* N of Cape San Vito.

14 March 1941 *Thunderbolt* sunk by depth-charges from Italian corvette *Cicogna* off Trapani.

31 March 1941 *Rorqual* sank the Italian submarine *Pier Capponi* south of Stromboli.

3 April 1941 *Tigris* sank German tanker *Thorn*.

10-14 April 1941 *Upholder* (ex-*P.37*, Lt Cdr Wanklyn) carried out several attacks on Axis ships off Cape Bon.

Left: *Captain G W G 'Shrimp' Simpson, who ran the 10th Submarine Flotilla at Malta during the hard days of 1941-42. He later served as FOSM, 1952-54.* (SMM)

Right: *Unidentified U-class at Malta.* (SMM)

12 April 1941	*Tetrarch* sank Italian tanker *Persiano* in Mediterranean.
26 April 1941	*Usk* (ex-*P.41*, Lt Darling) lost by unknown cause, probably mined, off Cape Bon.
April 1941	*Urge* (Lt Cdr Tomkinson) torpedoed Italian tanker *Franco Martelli* off Brest.
April 1941	*Truant* drove Italian naval auxiliary *Prometeo* ashore, where she became a total loss (exact date unknown).
6 May 1941	*Truant* sank Italian merchant ship *Bengasi*.
	Taku sank Italian merchant ship *Cagliari*.
12 May 1941	*Undaunted* (ex-*P.34*, Lt Cdr Livesay) sunk by unknown cause, probably mine, off Tripoli.
18 May 1941	*Tetrarch* sank Italian merchant ship *Giovenezza*.
24 May 1941	*Upholder* torpedoed the Italian troopship *Conte Rosso*, for which Wanklyn was awarded the Victoria Cross.
2 June 1941	*Union* (ex-*P.35*, Lt Galloway) torpedoed Italian merchant ship *Pietro Querini* S of Pantelleria.
6 June 1941	*Torbay* sank Italian tanker *Alberta*.
10 June 1941	*Torbay* sank Italian tanker *Ghirardi*.
11 June 1941	*Taku* sank the Italian merchant ship *Tilly Russ*.

12 June 1941   *Taku* sank the Italian merchant ship *Scaroni*.

25 June 1941   *Parthian* torpedoed Vichy French submarine *Souffleur* off Syrian coast.

27 June 1941   *Triumph* (Cdr Woods) sank Italian submarine *Salpa* with gunfire and torpedo off Mersa Matruh.

2 July 1941   *Torbay* sank the Italian merchant ship *Tripoli*.

5 July 1941   *Tigris* sank the Italian submarine *Michele Bianchi*.

Torbay sank the Italian submarine *Jantina* in the Aegean.

10 July 1941   *Torbay* damaged the Italian tanker *Strombo* beyond repair.

13 July 1941   *Taku* sank the Italian merchant ship *Caldea*.

15 July 1941   *P.33* (Lt Whiteway-Wikinson) sank Italian ship *Barbarigo* S of Pantelleria.

19 July 1941   *Umpire* (ex-P.31, Lt Cdr Wingfield) sunk in collision with Dutch trawler off the Wash. Five lives lost.

20 July 1941   *Union* depth-charged by Italian torpedo boat *Circe* SSW of Pantelleria.

30 July 1941	*Cachalot* (Lt Cdr Newton) rammed by Italian torpedo boat *Generale Achille Papa* off Benghazi. She was carrying stores and personnel from Malta to Alexandria. One life lost.
7 August 1941	*Tigris* sank the German merchant ship *Haakon Jarl*.
18 August 1941	*P.32* ('U' class, Lt Abdy) mined off Tripoli. Only two survivors.
	P.33 sunk off Tripoli, probably mined.
20 August 1941	*Trident* sank the German merchant ship *Ostpreussen*.

'S' class War Emergency and 1941 Programmes

These improved and enlarged developments of the *Shark* class had welded framing and were designed for operations in the North Sea. Thirty-three vessels were laid down during 1940-43 and completed 1942-45. Six of the class were not armed with the external TT and only carried 12 torpedoes. As an alternative 12 M2 mines could be carried instead of torpedoes. Several of the class were later armed with a 20mm gun. *Satyr*, *Spiteful*, *Sportsman* and *Statesman* were transferred to France in 1951-52.

'S' class Specifications (improved)

Displacement:	814-842/990tons
Dimensions:	217ft (oa) x 23ft 9in x 13ft 10in-14ft 8in (max)
Machinery:	2-shaft Vickers or Admiralty diesels, electric motors, 1900bhp/1300shp
Speed:	14.75/9kts
Armament:	7-21in TT (6 bow, 1 external) 13 torpedoes 1-3in (3 armed with 1-4in/40 cal Mk XII) gun
Complement:	48

HMS Seraph *on completion at the end of 1941.* (SMM)

Names to Numbers and Back to Names

Admiral Sir David Beatty, the First Sea Lord, advocated in 1925 that submarines should be named, as 'there can be little loyalty to a number'. Accordingly, the first post-war patrol submarines came into service with 'O' names, rather than the numbers allocated.

Soon after the outbreak of the Second World War the Hopwood Committee recommended a reversion to numbers to 'conceal the number of submarines being built', but the instigator was widely believed to be FOSM, Admiral Sir Max Horton. Names for new submarines were abandoned, instead 'P' numbers, corresponding to allocated pendant numbers, were used to identify vessels. This continued until late in 1942, when, according to hallowed tradition, Winston Churchill intervened, echoing the words of Admiral Beatty in the early 1920s, 'there can be no loyalty to a mere number. Names are important'. When the policy was reversed the numbered boats received appropriate class-names, but many were sunk before that was done.

Numbers allocated (with subsequent names):
P.31 (*Ulleswater*, then *Uproar*), *P.32*, *P.33*, *P.34* (*Ultimatum*), *P.35* (*Umbra*), *P.36*, *P.37* (*Unbending*), *P.38*, *P.39*, *P.41* (Norwegian *Uredd*), *P.42* (*Unbroken*), *P.43* (*Unison*), *P.44* (*United*), *P.45* (*Unrivalled*), *P.46* (*Unruffled*), *P.47*, *P.48*, *P.49* (*Unruly*), *P.51* (*Unseen*), *P.52*, *P.53* (*Ultor*), *P.54* (*Unshaken*), *P.55* (*Unsparing*), *P.56* (*Usurper*), *P.57* (*Universal*), *P.58* (*Vitality*), *P.64* (*Vandal*), *P.65* (*Untiring*, then *Upstart*), *P.222*, *P.311* (ex-*Tutankhamen*), *P.614* (ex-Turkish *Burak Reis*), *P.615* (ex-Turkish *Uluc Ali Reis*). In addition nine elderly submarines were transferred from the US Navy under Lend Lease: *P.511* (ex-*R.3*), *P.512* (ex-*R.7*), *P.514* (ex-*R.19*), *P.551* (ex-*S.25*, later Polish *Jastrzab*), *P.552* (ex-*S.1*), *P.553* (ex-*S.21*), *P.555* (ex-*S.24*), *P.556* (ex-*S.29*).

Four enemy submarines were captured:
U.570 (renamed *Graph*), *P.711* (ex-*X.2*, ex-Italian *Galileo Galilei*), *P.712* (ex-Italian *Perla*, later Greek *Matrozos*), *P.714* (ex-Italian *Bronzo*, later French *Narval*).

26 August 1941	*Triumph* laid a minefield which damaged the Italian heavy cruiser *Bolzano*.
30 August 1941	*Trident* sank the German merchant ship *Dona II*.
7 September 1941	*Thunderbolt* sank the Italian merchant ship *Sirena*.
11 September 1941	*Thunderbolt* sank the Italian merchant ship *Livorno*.
13 September 1941	*Tigris* sank unidentified merchant ship.
17 September 1941	*Tigris* sank unidentified merchant ship.
20 September 1941	Launch of *P.222*, the first of the 'S' class War Emergency and 1941 Programmes.
23 September 1941	*Triumph* sank German merchant ship *Luwsee*.
27 September 1941	*Tetrarch* sank Italian merchant ship *Citta di Bastia*.
	Trident sank unidentified merchant ship.

Upright (Lt Wraith) torpedoed Italian torpedo boat *Albatros* NW of Cape Rasocolmo.

4 October 1941	*Talisman* sank German liner *Theophile Gautier*.
8 October 1941	*Trident* damaged German U-boat *U.31*.
14 October 1941	*Tigris* sank two unidentified German merchant ships.
23 October 1941	*Truant* sank Italian merchant ship *Virginia S*.
25 October 1941	*Triumph* sank Italian merchant ship *Monrosa*.
27 October 1941	*Tetrarch* (Lt Cdr Greenway) lost by unknown cause, probably mined, SE of Sardinia. She was carrying fuel, stores and personnel to Malta. No survivors.
31 October 1941	*Truant* sank Italian tanker *Meteor*.
3 November 1941	*Trident* sank German escort trawler *Uj.1213*.
7 November 1941	*Trident* damaged unidentified merchant ship.
24 November 1941	*Triumph* sank Italian tug *Hercules*.
25 November 1941	*Thrasher* sank the Italian merchant ship *Attilio Deffenu*.
4 December 1941	*Trusty* sank Italian merchant ship *Eridano*.
6 December 1941	*Perseus* (Lt Cdr Nicolay) mined off Kephalonia. Only one survivor. Mining confirmed when wreck was located in 2000.
11 December 1941	*Truant* sank the Italian torpedo boat *Alcione*.
	Talisman sank the Italian merchant ship *Galitea*.
mid-December 1941	*Urge* damaged Italian battleship *Vittorio Veneto* with a single torpedo-hit.
20-24 December 1941	*H.31* (Lt Gibbs) lost from unknown cause, probably a mine, in Bay of Biscay, while trying to prevent breakout of German surface ships from Brest.
30 December 1941	*Thorn* sank the Italian tanker *Campina*.
31 December 1941	*Triumph* (Lt Huddart) lost from unknown cause, probably mined, off Cape Sounion.
5 January 1942	*Upholder* torpedoed and sank the Italian Cagni class submarine

Polyarnoe the Reindeer

When HMS *Trident*, under the command of Lieutenant Commander G M Sladen, arrived at the Polyarnoe base outside Murmansk on 10 August 1941 she was tasked with co-operating with the Soviet naval authorities by attacking the German troop convoys passing along the northern coast of Norway. As part of the ceremonies to mark the reconciliation between Great Britain and Soviet Russia in the face of the common foe, the Russians presented a young reindeer doe. Diplomatic protocol did not allow Sladen to refuse such a generous gesture.

Christened Polyarnoe in honour of the grim base allocated to the Royal Navy submarines and surface ships, the young reindeer seemed to adapt very quickly to the peculiar demands of life in submarines. It is recorded that Polyarnoe soon understood the importance of the CO in the pecking order, and followed his every move. If the *Trident* surfaced to open a hatch to ventilate the boat, Polyarnoe trotted to the foot of the ladder and looked up, clearly enjoying her brief spell of fresh air.

After *Trident*'s last patrol in February 1942, during which she hit the heavy cruiser *Prinz Eugen* with three torpedoes and blew off her stern, the time came to return home. Now a fresh problem became obvious. Polyarnoe had grown, not least because she was given rather more to eat than she needed by the sailors, and she could be described as 'spoilt rotten'. It seemed unlikely that she could be carried up a vertical ladder and out of a circular hatch without inflicting grave physical damage with her hooves and antlers. Accordingly when the submarine was close to home, a radio message was sent to solicit advice and assistance.

On the dockside, a man was waiting to give the aid and comfort required, but the submariners were appalled to learn that he was the slaughterman from the local abattoir. Mutiny loomed, but he explained that he had not come to slit Polyarnoe's throat, but to use his expertise to truss her securely until she was back on dry land. Polyarnoe seemed unshaken by her ordeal, but worked off her aggression by putting to flight a small dog walking innocently along the quay. Happily, Polyarnoe, after writing a very unusual chapter in the history of HM Submarines, ended her days in the local zoo.

Ammiraglio di Saint-Bon N of Sicily.

10 January 1942   *Thrasher* sank the Italian merchant ship *Fedora*.

12 January 1942   *Unbeaten* (Lt Woodward) torpedoed German U-boat *U.374* off Catania.

23 January 1942   *Thorn* (Lt Cdr Norfolk) sank Italian merchant ship *Ninnuccia* off Mljet in Adriatic.

30 January 1942   *Thorn* torpedoed Italian submarine *Medusa* off Pola.

1 February 1942   *Thunderbolt* sank the Italian merchant ship *Absirtea*.

12 February 1942   *Una* (Lt Martin) torpedoed Italian tanker *Lucania* in error (she had been granted a safe passage).

13 February 1942   *Tempest* (Lt Cdr Cavaye) damaged by depth-charges of Italian torpedo boat *Circe* in Gulf of Taranto and later sank in tow. 24 survivors.

16 February 1942   After sinking a supply ship, *Thrasher* was attacked by enemy aircraft, and two unexploded bombs lodged in the casing below the gun. The First Lieutenant, Lt Roberts, and PO Gould

Left: *Commander A C C Miers commanded HMS Torbay, and was awarded the Victoria Cross for an outstanding attack on shipping in Corfu Roads on 4-5 March 1942, when he spent 20 hours **inside** the anchorage, torpedoing two ships and still finding time to recharge batteries.* (SMM)

Right: *Lieutenant Commander Hugh 'Rufus' Macknezie, when CO of HMS Thrasher in 1942. Later he carried out two of the longest patrols in the war when commanding HMS Tantalus. Post-war he led the Polaris Executive, charged with getting the SSBNs built and operational, which he achieved on time and within cost.* (SMM)

volunteered to remove them; the first was comparatively easy, but the second was lying in a very confined space. Gould lay on his back with the bomb in his arms, and for 40 minutes Lt Roberts dragged him by his shoulders, until the bomb was clear and could be thrown over the side. Both men were awarded the VC.

23 February 1942   *P.38* ('U' class, Lt Hemingway) depth-charged by Italian torpedo boat *Circe* NW of Ras Misurata. No survivors.

Trident damaged the German heavy cruiser *Prinz Eugen*.

4-5 March 1942   *Torbay* sank the Italian merchant ship *Maddalena G* for which the CO Cdr Miers was awarded the VC.

14 March 1942   *Ultimatum* torpedoed the Italian submarine *Ammiraglio Millo* in Ionian Sea.

17 March 1942   *Unbeaten* torpedoed Italian submarine *Guglielmotti* off Calabria.

18 March 1942   *Upholder* torpedoed Italian submarine *Tricheco* off Brindisi.

26 March 1942   *P.39* ('U' class, Lt Marriott) bombed by German aircraft at Malta and written off as a constructive total loss.

1 April 1942   *Urge* sank the Italian light cruiser *Giovanni delle Bande Nere*.

Truant sank the Japanese merchant ships *Yae Maru* and *Shunsei Maru* in SE Asian waters.

Pandora (Lt Alexander) bombed by German aircraft in Sliema Creek, Malta. Raised in September 1943 and beached in Kalkara Creek; finally scrapped in 1955.

P.36 ('U' class, Lt Edmonds) bombed by German aircraft in Sliema Creek, Malta; raised in July 1958 and scuttled off Malta 22 August 1958.

9 April 1942   *Thrasher* sank the Italian merchant ship *Gala*.

13 April 1942   *Thrasher* sank the Italian merchant ship *Atlas*.

14 April 1942   *Upholder* depth-charged by Italian torpedo boat *Pegaso* N of Tripoli. No survivors.

16 April 1942   *Turbulent* sank the Italian merchant ship *Delia*.

18 April 1942   *Torbay* sank the Italian merchant ship *Bellona*.

20 April 1942   *Trident* sank the German merchant ship *Hoedur*.

29 April 1942   *Urge* (ex-*P.40*) bombed by Italian aircraft in Eastern Mediterranean after attacking tanker *San Giusto*.

HMS Safari *leaving HMS* Dolphin *in 1942 or 1943.*
(SMM)

Midgets, Chariots and Welmancraft

The success of the Italian *Maiale* ('pigs') in penetrating Alexandria harbour in December 1941 and severely damaging two battleships led to a virtual copy design. Known to the British as the 'Chariot', it was a two-man delivery vehicle, with a detachable warhead which could be clamped to the bottom of a target and detonated by a time fuze to allow the vehicle to escape. Although popularly known as 'human torpedoes', Chariots were simply slow vehicles driven by electric motors, and were not converted 'tin fish'.

Welman craft were small midget submarines designed by an Army officer, Colonel Dolphin, and with the Welfreighter semi-submersible cargo-carrier and swimmer-delivery vehicles, were used in Norway, where many were manned by Norwegians, but they had only limited success.

A former submariner, Cdr Varley, started development of a small submarine for use in rivers by the Army in 1939, and his persistent nagging of the Admiralty paid off when the need to penetrate defended anchorages became apparent. The battleship *Tirpitz* was the objective, for it was important to prevent her from emerging from her base in the Norwegian fjords to attack convoys heading for North Russia.

Two prototypes, *X.3* and *X.4*, were built by Varley Marine in 1941-42, with assistance from Portsmouth Dockyard, and *X.5-10* were ordered from Vickers Armstrongs' Barrow in Furness yard. In addition six training boats, *XT.1-6*, were built by Vickers Armstrong (*XT.14-19* cancelled). For the Far East a slightly larger and more habitable design was needed, and *XE.1-12* were ordered from Broadbent Markham of Chesterfield and Marshall of Gainsborough (*XE.10* was subsequently cancelled).

The X-craft carried two 2-ton time-fuzed side charges which could be released from inside the submarine and dropped under the keel of the target. They were towed to the scene of operations by 'S' or 'T' class boats, to save their batteries and to rest their crews. Serious damage was done to *Tirpitz* by X-craft and to the Japanese heavy cruiser *Takao* by an XE-craft.

The midget XE.9 seen about 1945, one of nine built with air-conditioning and other refinements for Far East operations. She and XE.8 survived until 1953, when both were sold for scrap. (SMM)

The Welfreighter was not, strictly speaking, a submarine, but a semi-submersible carrier for combat swimmers. (SMM)

Another view of a Welfreighter, which took its name, like the one-man Welman midget, from the town of Welwyn, where they were built. (SMM)

Midget XE.5 alongside HMS Selene in the Far East. (BAES Marine)

Hoisting a 'Chariot' over the side. (Author's collection)

The old depot ship
Titania, *with* L.23
*alongside, with a
cylindrical container for
transporting Chariots
welded on the casing for
training.* (NPC)

The midget X.24 *being
prepared for display at
the Royal Navy
Submarine Museum.*
(SMM)

XT.1, *one of six training
midgets, less elaborately
equipped than the
operational X-craft. They
were built at Barrow.*
(BAES Marine)

David Wanklyn and HMS *Upholder*

Lt Cdr M D Wanklyn joined the newly completed *Upholder* in August 1940, and sailed for the Mediterranean via Gibraltar in December. She arrived at Malta on 12 January 1941, and berthed in Lazaretto Creek alongside the former quarantine hospital, which served as the HQ of the submarine flotilla, HMS *Talbot*.

Malta was already feeling the effects of German and Italian air raids, and ammunition, torpedoes and spares were in short supply. Ten 'U' class boats were based there, the larger boats having been withdrawn to Alexandria. HMS *Upholder*'s first patrol saw the claimed destruction of only one merchant ship, believed to be the German Duisburg (8000 tons).

Part of the newly formed 10th Submarine Flotilla from June 1941, she sank no ships on the second, third and fourth patrols, but on the fifth she sank the merchant ship *Antonietta Laura*, finished off the stranded *Arta* and sank a German merchant ship, the *Leverkusen*. On 24 May, during her seventh patrol, she sank the troopship *Conte Rosso*, an exploit which won Wanklyn the VC.

Wanklyn was given a rest period in June 1941, being relieved temporarily by Lt Hezlet. Two days after returning from her 12th patrol, *Upholder* was sent to intercept a troop convoy, and on 17 September she sank the *Neptunia* and *Oceania*. During the 17th patrol she sank the destroyer *Libeccio* and damaged another, but failed to sink a submarine. During the 20th patrol she sank the submarine *Ammiraglio di Saint-Bon*. When she was sunk on her final 25th patrol she had sunk a claimed total of 119,000 tons, making her the top-scoring Royal Navy submarine.

Lt Cdr Wanklyn proved to be a dedicated leader, who refused to allow periods of zero success and bad luck weaken his resolve. His quiet confidence created and maintained strong morale, and although he must have been under great mental strain, this never showed.

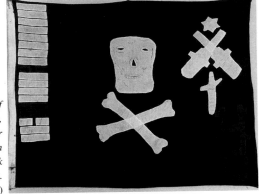

Lt Cdr David Wanklyn VC, the most successful Royal Navy submariner of the Second World War, with some 90,000 ton of Axis shipping sunk. (SMM)

The Jolly Roger of HMS Upholder, *showing bars for ships sunk, a gun action and a 'cloak and dagger' mission. (Author's collection)*

The only known photograph of HMS Upholder *(outboard), with* Urge *inboard, taken at Malta in 1941 or early 1942. (Author's collection)*

'T' class, 1941 and 1942 Programmes

A further development of the 1940 'T' class programme, these 22 vessels were laid down during 1941-42 for completion in 1943-46. These later boats had welded fuel tanks and hull plating, and several were fitted with air-conditioning for operations in the Pacific. Two, *Talent* and *Tarn*, were transferred to the Royal Netherlands Navy in 1943 and 1945 as the *Zwaardvis* and *Tijgerhaai* respectively. The 1942 programme boats had thicker plating, permitting them to dive to 350ft (test-dived to 400ft). Five cancelled in 1945.

During the Second World War the 'Ts' proved their worth, operating in all the theatres sinking large numbers of enemy warships and mercantile targets. Modern authorities point to the success of the 'Ts' in the Mediterranean as proof of the fallacy that medium-displacement boats were too vulnerable. It is argued that building so many 'Us' was a mistake, and the resources would have been better spent on more 'Ts'.

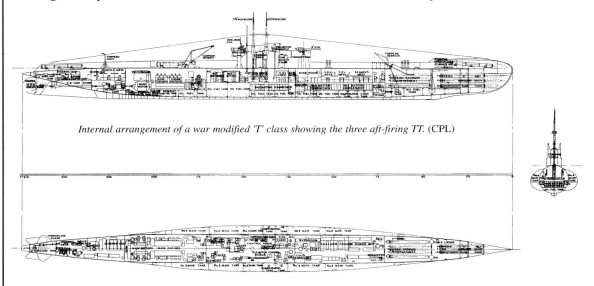

Internal arrangement of a war modified 'T' class showing the three aft-firing TT. (CPL)

8 May 1942 *Olympus* (Lt Cdr Dymott) mined off Malta with 90 survivors (she had numerous additional personnel on board, including crew-members of the sunken *P.36*, *P.39* and *Pandora*).

18 May 1942 *Turbulent* sank the Italian merchant ship *Bolsena*.

19 May 1942 *Thrasher* sank the Italian merchant ship *Penelope*.

29 May 1942 *Turbulent* sank the Italian destroyer *Emanuele Pessagno* and the merchant ship *Capo Arma*.

4 June 1942 *Trusty* sank the Japanese merchant ship *Toyohashi Maru* in SE Asian waters.

15 June 1942 *Umbra* hit the Italian battleship *Littorio* with single torpedo, and then sank the damaged heavy cruiser *Trento*.

21 June 1942 *P.514* (ex-USS *R.19*, Lt Cdr Pain) rammed in error by Canadian minesweeper HMCS *Georgian* while heading from Argentina to

'T' class Specifications (further improved)

Displacement:	319-27/1567-1571 tons
Dimensions:	273ft 3in-273ft 6in (oa) x 26ft 7in x 14ft 8in-14ft 10in (max)
Machinery:	2-shaft Vickers or Admiralty diesels, electric motors, 2500bhp/1450shp
Speed:	15.25/9kts
Armament:	11-21in TT (6 bow, 5 external) 17 torpedoes
	1-4in 40 cal Mk XII gun (Mk XXII in 6vessels)
	1-20mm AA gun
Complement:	61

A late 'T', possibly Talent *(ex-*Tasman*) in 1945, with all the war improvements, including an external stern torpedo-tube and angled aft-firing tubes.*
(BAES Marine)

St John, Newfoundland. No survivors.

23 June 1942   *Thrasher* sank the Italian merchant ship *San Antonio*.

24 June 1942   *Turbulent* sank the Italian merchant ship *Regulus*.

29 June 1942   *Thrasher* torpedoed Italian sloop *Diana*.

3 August 1942   *Thorn* sank the Italian merchant ship *Monviso*.

       Saracen (Lt Lumby) torpedoed German U-boat *U.335* NE of Shetlands.

7 August 1942   *Thorn* depth-charged by Italian torpedo boat *Pegaso* SW of Gavdo Island. No survivors.

4 September 1942   *Thrasher* sank the Italian merchant ship *Padenna*.

5 September 1942   *Traveller* sank the Italian merchant ship *Albachirar*.

HMS Seraph, *completed early in 1942, was one of only three 'S' class built at Barrow, most of the others being built at Birkenhead.* (BAES Marine)

17 September 1942	*Talisman* (Lt Cdr Willmott) lost by unknown cause, probably mined, in Sicilian Channel.
23 September 1942	Launch of *Tudor*, the first of the 1941 and 1942 programme improved 'T' class.
8 October 1942	*Turbulent* sank the Italian merchant ship *Kreta*.
19 October 1942	*Seraph* (Lt Jewell) left Gibraltar carrying US General Mark Clark and his staff to Algeria, to negotiate with the French pro-Vichy forces in North Africa. On her return on 25 October *Seraph* was ordered to undertake another clandestine mission, this time to persuade General Giraud to join the Allies. Giraud refused to be 'rescued' by a British submarine, so *Seraph* was temporarily placed under the command of Captain Jerauld Wright USN, and flew the Stars and Stripes.
	Unbending torpedoed Italian destroyer *Giovanni da Verrazano*.
20 October 1942	*Thrasher* sank the Italian merchant ship *Lero*.
23 October 1942	*Unique* (ex-*P.36*, Lt Boddington) lost from unknown cause, possibly depth-charged, W of Gibraltar.
26 October 1942	*Taku* sank the Italian tanker *Arca*.
4 November 1942	*X.3* (Sub Lt Lorimer) lost while exercising in Loch Striven.

Lieutenant Jewell and officers and lookouts on the bridge of HMS Seraph. The X-shaped antenna of the Type 267 airguard radar set is at the after end of the conning tower. Note the Ferdinand the Bull logo on the front of the conning tower, an oblique reference to her several clandestine missions. (SMM)

Officers and ratings of HMS Seraph display their Jolly Roger. (SMM)

HMS Sceptre *on the Clyde, possibly running trials in 1943, as she has all the wartime 'extras' including radar and the 20mm Oerlikon gun. (SMM)*

9 November 1942   *Saracen* torpedoed the Italian submarine *Granito* off Cape San Vito, Sicily.

11 November 1942   *Unbeaten* (ex-*P.33*, Lt Watson) bombed in error in Bay of Biscay by RAF Wellington bomber.

Turbulent sank the Italian naval auxiliary *Benghazi*.

25 November 1942   *Utmost* (ex-*P.42*, Lt Coombe) depth-charged by Italian torpedo boat *Groppo* NW of Marittimo. No survivors. A day earlier she had attacked the Italian auxiliary cruiser *Barletta* unsuccessfully but in her short career she had already sunk nearly 70,000 tons of shipping.

4 December 1942   *Traveller* (Lt Cdr St Clair Ford) lost from unknown cause, probably mined, off Taranto. She had been reconnoitring the approaches to the main Italian base as a prelude to a 'Chariot' attack by *Thunderbolt*, *Trooper* and *P.311*.

6 December 1942   *Tigris* sank the Italian submarine *Porfido* of Bône, near Algeria.

12 December 1942   *P.222* ('S' class, ex-*P.72*, Lt Cdr Mackenzie) depth-charged by Italian destroyer *Fortunale* off Naples. No survivors.

14 December 1942   *Taku* sank the Italian merchant ship *Delfin*.

17 December 1942   *Splendid* sank the Italian destroyer *Aviere*.

25 December 1942   *P.48* ('U' class) depth-charged by Italian corvette *Ardente* NW of Zembra Island.

29 December 1942   *Turbulent* sank the Italian merchant ship *Marte*.

2 January 1943   *P.311* (ex-*Tutankhamen*, ex-*P.91*, Lt Cdr Cayley) lost, probably mined, off Maddalena. She had been converted to carry 'Chariots' in deck-cylinders, and was taking part in a planned attack on Taranto.

3 January 1943   'Chariots' sank the Italian light cruiser *Ulpio Traiano*, fitting out at Palermo.

11 January 1943   *Turbulent* sank the Italian merchant ship *Beraldo*.

  Tribune sank the Italian merchant ship *Dalny*.

17 January 1943   *United* torpedoed Italian destroyer *Bombardiere*.

21 January 1943   *Tigris* sank the Italian merchant ship *Citta di Genova*.

1 February 1943   *Turbulent* sank the Italian merchant ship *Pozzuoli*.

5 February 1943   *Turbulent* sank the Italian tanker *Utilitas*.

11 February 1943   *Torbay* sank the Italian merchant ship *Grete*.

24 February 1943   *Vandal* (Lt Bridger) lost in Kilbrannan Sound, presumably after a diving accident. No survivors.

26 February 1943   *Torbay* sank the Italian merchant ships *Astigarraga*.

27 February 1943   *Tigris* (Lt Cdr Colvin) depth-charged by German trawler *Uj.2210* S of Capri.

Two Chariots with their cylindrical containers welded to the after casing of HMS Trooper. *The right hand Chariot is fully withdrawn from the cylinder while the left hand one is partially withdrawn showing the rails.* (SMM)

HMS Unshaken *in a Mediterranean port, possibly Algiers.* (SMM)

28 February 1943   *Torbay* sank the Italian merchant ship *Ischia.*

1 March 1943   *Turbulent* sank the Italian merchant ship *San Vincenzo.*

6 March 1943   *Taurus* sank the Italian merchant ship *Bartolo.*

10 March 1943   *Taurus* sank the Italian merchant ship *Derna.*

         Trooper sank the Italian tanker *Rosario.*

12 March 1943   *Thunderbolt* (ex-*Thetis,*) sank the Italian merchant ship *Esterel.* *Thunderbolt* was then depth-charged by Italian corvette *Cicogna* N of Cape San Vito. She was a 'Chariot' carrier, and had taken part in the abortive attack on Taranto.

c17 March 1943   *Turbulent* (Cdr Linton) sunk, probably by mine, off Corsica. Linton sank some 30 ships totalling 100,000 tons, for which he was awarded the DSO, and was posthumously awarded the VC.

17 March 1943   *Trooper* sank the Italian merchant ship *Forli.*

28 March 1943   *Torbay* sank the merchant ship *Lillois.*

7 April 1943   *Tuna* (Lt Cdr Martin) torpedoed German U-boat *U.644* S of Jan Mayen Island. A week later she attacked *U.302*, but without success.

14 April 1943   *Taurus* sank the Italian tanker *Alcione C.*

18 April 1943	*P.615* (ex-Turkish *Uluc Ali Reis*, Lt Lambert) torpedoed by German U-boat *U.123* off Freetown.

18 April 1943 *P.615* (ex-Turkish *Uluc Ali Reis*, Lt Lambert) torpedoed by German U-boat *U.123* off Freetown.

Regent (Lt Knox) mined in Straits of Otranto.

21 April 1943 *Splendid* (ex-*P.78*, Lt McGeoch) depth-charged by German destroyer *Hermes* off W coast of Corsica.

24 April 1943 *Sahib* (ex-*P.62*, Lt Bromage) depth-charged by Italian corvette *Gabbiano* N of Sicily.

28 April 1943 *Unshaken* torpedoed Italian torpedo boat *Climene*.

29 April 1943 *Seraph* dropped the corpse of the 'Man Who never Was' ('Major Martin'), in the sea off the Huelva River in Spain, as part of the deception plan for the invasion of Sicily.

4 May 1943 Launch of *Venturer*, the first of the 1941 'long hull' and 1942 'U' class programmes.

30 May 1943 *Untamed* (Lt Noll) lost with all hands in diving accident during exercise off Sanda Island. Raised and returned to service as *Vitality*.

4 June 1943 *Truculent* sank the German U-boat *U.307*.

14 June 1943 *United* sank merchant ship *Ringulv*.

Tactician sank the Italian merchant ship *Rosandra*.

13 July 1943 *Unruly* torpedoed Italian submarine *Accaio* N of Messina Straits.

15 July 1943 Unidentified RN submarine torpedoed Italian submarine *Remo* in Gulf of Salerno.

23 July 1943 *Torbay* sank the Italian merchant ship *Aderno*.

29 July 1943 *Trooper* torpedoed Italian submarine *Pietro Micca* in Straits of Otranto.

7 August 1943 *Parthian* (Lt Pardoe) sunk, probably by mine, off Brindisi.

9 August 1943 *Simoom* torpedoed Italian destroyer *Vincenzo Gioberti*.

14 August 1943 *Saracen* (ex-*P.427*) depth-charged by Italian corvette *Minerva* off Bastia.

2 September 1943 *Torbay* sank the Italian merhant ship *Versilia*.

'U' class 1941 'long hull' and 1942 programmes.

In 1941 a 'long hull' improved 'U' class design, referred to as the 'V' class, was prepared incorporating an improved hullform and an increased length of 206ft (oa) due to the adoption of a 'shark' bowform. This decreased noise by changing the angle of water approaching the propeller. The hulls of this class were welded and the riveted plating was increased from .5in to .75in giving a diving depth of 300ft. The class was intended to run to 42 units all built by Vickers at Barrow and on the Tyne, but 20 were cancelled at the end of the war in 1945. *Variance*, in 1944, *Venturer*, *Viking* and *Votary*, in 1946, were transferred to the Norwegian Navy.

'U' class & 'V' class Specifications

Displacement:	658-662/740tons
Dimensions:	204ft 6in (oa) x 16ft 1in x 15ft 3in (max)
Machinery:	2-shaft Paxman diesels, electric motors, 615bhp/825shp
Speed:	11.25/10kts
Armament:	4-21in TT (bow) 8 torpedoes 1-3in
Complement:	33

Despite her 'U' name, HMS Upshot *was a 'V' class boat completed by Vickers in 1944.* (BAES Marine)

The 'V' class was an improved 'U', distinguishable by the low 'shark' bow. This is probably Varne, *in Holy Loch in 1944-45.* (BAES Marine)

X-Craft against the *Tirpitz*

In the early days of January 1943, *X.5*, *X.6*, *X.7*, *X.8*, *X.9* and *X.10*, accompanied by their depot ship *Bonaventure*, arrived at Loch Cairnbawn to begin intensive training. Their task was to implement an order from Winston Churchill to attack the German battleship *Tirpitz* in her hiding place in Kaafjord, in Northern Norway. There she was almost invulnerable to air attack because of the high cliffs and able to reach the open sea at very short notice to attack the convoys heading for North Russia. It was an old naval problem, trying to bring a reluctant enemy to action, but the X-craft were inspired by the Italians' successful penetration of Alexandria at the end of 1941.

As the X-craft were too small to accommodate torpedo-tubes, they relied on 2-ton side charges which could be dropped under the target. They would be towed to the scene of operations by normal submarines, with passage-crews to allow the operational crew to rest. On 11 September HMS *Truculent* sailed with *X.6* in tow, followed by *Syrtis* with *X.9*, *Thrasher* with *X.10*, *Seanymph* with *X.8*, *Stubborn* with *X.7* and *Sceptre* with *X.10*. Four days later trouble began when *X.8* was forced to jettison her side-charges and *X.9*'s towline broke (she was never seen again). By 6pm on 20 September, the surviving midgets, *X.5* (Lt Henty-Creer RNVR), *X.6* (Lt Cameron RN), *X.7* (Lt Place RN) and *X.10* (Lt Hudspeth RANVR), were ready to slip their tows and head for the outer minefield which protected Kaafjord.

The attack was a great success, immobilising the *Tirpitz* and eventually forcing the *Kriegsmarine* to move her to a southern fjord to allow major repairs. There she was within range of bombers operating from bases in Britain, and she was duly sunk in 1944, the last seagoing German capital ship. The price paid by the X-craft was heavy: *X.5* was sunk without reaching the *Tirpitz*, *X.6* was scuttled after she laid her charges, *X.7* sank on her way out, and *X.10* was scuttled before the attack started. When the war was over, Lt Donald Cameron and Lt Godfrey Place were awarded the Victoria Cross, but Lt Henty-Creer's family started a long campaign to try to prove that *X.5* had carried out an attack on the *Tirpitz* and therefore also deserved a VC, something the Admiralty never accepted. The most recent effort to find the wreck of *X.5* failed to solve the mystery.

7 September 1943   *Shakespeare* torpedoed the Italian submarine *Velella* in the Gulf of Salerno.

16 September 1943   *X.9* lost on passage to Norway, in abortive attack on *Scharnhorst*.

18 September 1943   *X.8* scuttled on passage to Norway, in abortive attack on *Lützow*.

X.24 flying a Jolly Roger, indicating a successful mission. Under Lieutenant Sheean RANVR she sank the German blockade-runner Barenfels *on 14 April 1944. Under Lieutenant Westmacott RN she returned to Bergen and put a floating dock out of action on 11 September 1944. (SMM)*

'S' class 1942 and 1943 Programmes

Similar to the 1941 'S' class, these 17 vessels were laid down during 1942-44 with completion in 1943-45. *Sturdy* and *Stygian* were essentially 1941 class boats, with a depth limit of 300ft, the other vessels in the class had welded pressure hull plating providing them with a depth limit of 350ft. *Sturdy*, *Stygian* and *Subtle* had an external stern TT, while all the boats of the class could carry 12 M2 mines instead of torpedoes. All were later armed with a 20mm gun. *Spearhead*, *Saga* and *Spur* were transferred to the Portuguese Navy in 1948, while *Springer* and *Sanguine* entered Israeli service in 1958.

'S' class Specifications

Displacement:	814-842/990tons
Dimensions:	217ft (oa) x 23ft 9in x 13ft 11in-14ft 8in (max)
Machinery:	2-shaft Admiralty diesels, electric motors, 1900bhp/1300shp
Speed:	14.75/9kts
Armament:	7-21in TT (bow) 12 torpedoes
	1-4in/40 cal Mk XII gun
Complement:	48

HMS Stonehenge *in the Mersey after completion in 1943. Note the direction-finding (D/F) loop on the after casing, abaft the conning tower platform and its 20mm Oerlikon gun. (SMM)*

HMS Storm, *on her return to Portsmouth from the Far East in 1945. (SMM)*

22 September 1943 *X.5* sunk in Altenfjord by unknown cause during the approach to the berth of the *Tirpitz*.

X.6 sunk in Altenfjord.

X.7 sunk in Altenfjord. Salved 1976 and preserved.

30 September 1943 Launch of *Sturdy*, the first vessel of the 1942 and 1943 programme 'S' class.

3 October 1943 *X.10* scuttled in the North Sea after an abortive attack on the *Scharnhorst*.

Usurper (ex-*P.56* Lt Mott) depth-charged by German anti-submarine vessel *Uj.2208* in the Gulf of Genoa.

10 October 1943 *Trooper* (Lt Wraith) lost by unknown cause, probably mined, E of Leros.

16 October 1943 *Torbay* sank the merchant ship *Kari*.

The big depot ship HMS Adamant *late in the Second World War, with three 'T's (nearest to camera) and three 'Vs' alongside.* (SMM)

10 November 1943   *Tally Ho* sank the Japanese merchant ship *Kisogawa Maru*.

13 November 1943   *Taurus* sank the Japanese submarine *I.34*.

19 November 1943   *Simoom* (Lt Milner) torpedoed by German U-boat *U.565* off Dodecanese.

22 November 1943   *Torbay* sank a 15,000-ton floating dock, the largest target sunk by a 'T' boat.

Welman 45, 46, 47 and *48* lost in attack on Bergen.

27 November 1943   *Torbay* sank the merchant ship *Palma*.

7 January 1944   *Taku* sank the German merchant ship *Rheinhausen*.

11 January 1944   *Tally Ho* sank the Japanese light cruiser *Kuma*.

15 January 1944   *Tally Ho* sank the Japanese merchant ship *Ryuko Maru*.

'T' class boats of the 8th Submarine Flotilla outboard of the depot ship HMS Adamant, *moored alongside North Wharf, at Fremantle in Western Australia. This was the largest Allied submarine base in the Southern Hemisphere in 1942-45. (Vic Jeffery)*

27 January 1944   *Templar* sank the Japanese light cruiser *Kitakami*.

7 February 1944   *X.22* sunk in collision with *Syrtis* in Pentland Firth.

12 February 1944   *Taku* drove the German merchant ship *Fritzen* ashore. Next day she sank the *Bornhofen*.

14/15 February 1944   *Tally Ho* torpedoed German U-boat *UIT.23* (ex-Italian *Reginaldo Giuliani*) in Malacca Straits. The Italian boat had been used to transport high-value cargoes from Japan to Occupied Europe, and was seized at Singapore by the Japanese at the time of the Italian surrender, and handed over to the Germans.

21 February 1944   *Tally Ho* sank the Japanese merchant ship *Daigen Maru No.6*.

20 March 1944   *Stonehenge* (Lt Verschoyle-Campbell) lost from unknown cause off Nicobar Islands.

           Graph (ex-*U-570*) wrecked West of Islay while on her way to be used for depth-charge trials.

24 March 1944   *Terrapin* sank the German merchant ship *Werth* and the naval auxiliary *Schwabenwald*.

28 March 1944   *Truculent* sank the Japanese merchant ship *Yasushima Maru*.

           Syrtis (Lt Jupp) mined off Bodo, in N Norway.

22 April 1944   *Taurus* sank the Japanese naval auxiliary *Gio Hokuan*.

Royal Navy submariners at a dance held in their honour at Fremantle, WA in 1944. Some are in winter rig, others in summer rig. (Vic Jeffery)

The 'A' Class

In 1943 work started on a new class of boats intended for operations in the Far East, with emphasis on habitability, range and maximum torpedo stowage. Only 16 were completed in 1945-48, none of which saw wartime service, and 30 were cancelled. Their .75in welded pressure hulls were designed to dive to 500ft, with a test dive depth of 600ft. They were generally successful, but displayed a tendency to roll which was cured by adding a bow buoyancy tank (reminiscent of the 'swan' bow in the 'K' class three decades earlier). All were intended to have a 'snort' mast.

'A' class Specifications

Displacement:	1385/1620 tons
Dimensions:	279ft 3in (oa) x 22ft 3in x 17ft 1in
Machinery:	2-shaft Vickers or Admiralty supercharged diesels, electric motors, 4300bhp/1250shp
Speed:	18.5/8kts
Armament:	10-21in TT (4 bow, 2 stern, 4 external) 30 Mk VIII torpedoes 1-4in 40 cal Mk XII gun, 1-20mm AA gun
Complement:	61

HMS Aurochs *on trials. The triple periscope standards were the hallmark of the 'A' class, as well as the prominent bow (modified in the earliest units). (BAES Maritime)*

27 April 1944	*Taurus* sank the Japanese submarine *I.37*.
3 May 1944	*Tantalus* sank the Japanese merchant ship *Amagi Maru*.
12 May 1944	*Trespasser* sank the Japanese merchant ship *Kasumi Maru*.
18 May 1944	*Templar* damaged the Japanese merchant ship *Nichiyoku Maru* beyond repair.
23 May 1944	*Sceptre* (Lt McIntosh) sank the German blockade-running ore-carrier *Baldur* in Spanish territorial waters, provoking a minor diplomatic incident.
28 May 1944	*Templar* sank the Japanese merchant ship *Tyokai Maru*.
4 June 1944	*X.20* and *X.23* acted as beach markers off 'Sword' beach in preparation for the D-Day landings.
10 June 1944	*Tantalus* sank the Japanese merchant ship *Hyoshi Maru*.

HMS Astute *was completed by Vickers in 1945, too late to see war service. She and her sisters were designed for Pacific operations, with greater range, air-conditioning and other refinements.* (BAES Marine)

Internal arrangements of 'A' class with the snort mast. (John Lambert/CPL)

Four 'A' class fitting out at Barrow in 1945. Ten were delivered by Barrow, and 11 more cancelled. (BAES Marine)

c16 June 1944	*Sickle* (Lt Drummond) lost from unknown cause, probably air attack, in Antikithera Channel.
21 June 1944	Unidentified Royal Navy submarine torpedoed German torpedo boat *TA.25* (ex-Italian *Intrepido*). 'Chariots' sank the damaged Italian heavy cruiser *Bolzano* at La Spezia.
26 June 1944	'Chariots' sank the damaged Italian heavy cruiser *Gorizia* at La Spezia.
	Truculent sank the Japanese merchant ship *Harukiku Maru*.
17 July 1944	*Telemachus* sank the Japanese submarine *I.166*.
27 July 1944	*Sunfish* lent to Soviet Navy as *V.1* (the often-quoted *B.1* is a transliteration error) and sunk in error by RAF aircraft off N Norway. *B.2*, *B.3* and *B.4* transferred at the same time.
31 August 1944	*Amphion* (ex-*Anchorite*) launched at Barrow in Furness, first of a new design intended for the Pacific.
5 September 1944	*Tantivy* sank the Japanese merchant ship *Shiretoko Maru*.
18 September 1944	*Tradewind* sank the Japanese merchant ship *Junyo Maru*.
23 September 1944	*Trenchant* sank the German U-boat *U.859*.
October 1944	*Vulpine* fitted with a dummy snort mast to train RAF Coastal Command aircrews.

HMS Vulpine, *fitted with a dummy 'snort' for training Coastal Command air crews.* (SMM)

THE SECOND WORLD WAR

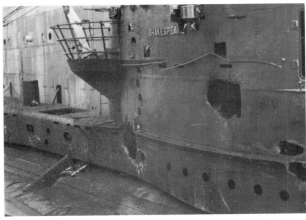

Bomb and splinter damage to HMS Shakespeare *after her near-disastrous engagement with Japanese aircraft off the Nicobar Islands in January 1945.* (SMM)

Leading Seaman Magennis (left) and Lieutenant Fraser (right) waiting to receive their VCs. (SMM)

6 October 1944   *Tally Ho* sank the Japanese *Submarine Chaser No.4* with gunfire in the Malacca Strait.

2 November 1944   *Tantalus* sank the Japanese merchant ship *Hachijin Maru*.

4 November 1944   *Terrapin* sank the Japanese *Special Minesweeper No.5*.

11 November 1944   *Venturer* sank *U.771*.

20 November 1944   *Tally Ho* sank the Japanese *Special Minelayer No.4*.

22 November 1944   *Stratagem* (Lt Pelly) depth-charged by Japanese patrol craft in Malacca Straits. On 18 November she had sunk the Japanese tanker *Nichinan Maru*.

3 January 1945   *Shakespeare* bombed and badly damaged by Japanese aircraft in Nankauri Strait; written off as constructive total loss.

19 January 1945   *Porpoise* (Lt Turner) bombed by Japanese aircraft off Penang.

9 February 1945   *Venturer* sank *U.864*, the only engagement in history between two submerged submarines. *Venturer* detected the U-boat, using her Type 129 Asdic in passive mode, foreshadowing modern anti-submarine tactics.

11 February 1945   *Tradewind* sank the Japanese merchant ship *Nanshin Maru*.

3 March 1945   *Sealion* scuttled as Asdic target.

4 March 1945   *Terrapin* and *Trenchant* sank the Japanese *Special Submarine Chaser No.5*.

HMS Turpin *(left) and*
HMS Tapir *alongside*
North Wharf in
Fremantle, WA in 1945.
(Vic Jeffery)

6 March 1945 XE.11 sunk in collision with a boom defence vessel in Loch Striven.

12 April 1945 *Tapir* sank the German U-boat *U.486.*

29 April 1945 *Tradewind* sank the Japanese tanker *Takasago Maru.*

9 May 1945 *Terrapin* badly damaged by Japanese patrol craft's depth-charges in S Pacific; declared a constructive total loss.

25 May 1945 *Thorough* sank the Japanese merchant ship *Nittei Maru.*

Trenchant sank the Japanese *Special Minesweeper No.105.*

1 June 1945 *Tiptoe* sank the Japanese merchant ship *Tobi Maru.*

8 June 1945 *Trenchant* (Cdr Hezlet) sank the Japanese heavy cruiser *Ashigara* off Sumatra.

Opposite:
Hulls and sections of 'A'
class boats being mass-
produced at Barrow at the
end of the Second World
War. (BAES Marine)

31 July 1945 XE.3 (Lt Fraser) damaged beyond repair the Japanese heavy cruiser *Takao* in Singapore. Fraser and Leading Seaman Magennis were both awarded VCs.

AND

CHAPTER 5

PEACE, COLD WAR, PEACE ONCE MORE
1945-2001

T HE WAR-WEARY NATIONS OF EUROPE hoped that a new era of peace had dawned with the defeat of Nazi Germany in 1945, but all too soon it became obvious that new tensions and rivalries had surfaced. It was also all too clear that the economies of Europe were so badly damaged that massive aid from outside would be needed to rebuild them.

Fortunately the United States Government accepted the recommendations of the wartime Chairman of the Joint Chiefs of Staff, General George C Marshall, and set in train the Marshall Plan to provide assistance to the countries of Europe. This was a major factor in countering Communist attempts at subverting Western Europe as easily as it had been done in Eastern Europe. For his part, Stalin showed little interest in rebuilding Eastern Europe, not least because the Soviet Union's industrial base had been seriously damaged by nearly four years of very destructive fighting.

It soon became clear, however, that Stalin was not content to defend his gains in Eastern Europe, and wanted to undermine the United States' influence in Europe. Europe was in no position to defend itself, and only a strong alliance, to which the United States was totally committed, could hope to deter the Soviet Union. This was the North Atlantic Treaty Organisation (NATO), so-called because it involved Canada and Great Britain as well as the United States, with a guarantee to the rest of the partners that an attack on one was an attack on all. At first NATO was little more than a paper organisation, but in the 1950s a fully-fledged command structure emerged, using English as the common language. Originally based at Fontainebleau in France to acknowledge France's role as the second most important European ally, it was forced to move to Brussels when President de Gaulle withdrew France from the military structure after a difference of opinion with the United States.

Outside NATO, the United States pursued a policy of containment through a series of regional alliances, and as in Europe, reinforced by the threat of a nuclear response. In fact, the nuclear deterrent was the only alternative to raising large conscript armies to match the strength of the Red Army. At first nuclear strategy was envisaged as instantaneous response to any threat, a scenario in which it was assumed that navies would play no part. A measure of common sense then reasserted itself, and navies were graciously awarded a secondary role in the 'broken-backed phase' following a nuclear exchange.

The obsession with strategic nuclear bombing, later superseded by the Intercontinental Ballistic Missile (ICBM), played havoc with naval planning in the late 1940s. Ship construction was slowed down, on the pretext that nobody could possibly know what sort of ships to build. The strategic bombing lobby, led by the US Air Force's Strategic Air Command (SAC) and abetted by the Royal Air Force, enjoyed so much prestige and credibility they succeeded in killing off the US Navy's planned aircraft carrier, the *United States* (CV-58) in 1949.

What saved navies from death by benign neglect was the Korean War, which broke out in 1950 when Communist North Korea invaded its pro-Western southern neighbour. Weak American land forces and the South Korean Army were brushed aside, and the only way to stop the North Korean Army from was by close air support from US Navy aircraft carriers. Later Royal Navy and Australian carriers arrived to take some of the load, and a Commonwealth Brigade and various allied detachments supplemented the US Amy reinforcements. Furthermore, General Douglas MacArthur's risky but inspired strategic realignment of the US forces by the amphibious landings at Inchon, 15 September 1950, reminded strategists of the inherent advantages that navies could provide in conventional war. Although no clear-cut tactical victory was won in Korea, Stalin and the Chinese

Previous pages:
HMS Dreadnought
leaving Faslane in April
1974 for a refit at
Chatham.
(Author's collection)

leader Mao Tse Tung had been shown that the Western Alliance would fight if provoked, and that it could not be swamped by sheer numbers alone. For Western navies it was also a timely reminder of the flexibility of conventional naval forces.

The value of the big aircraft carrier was now firmly established in naval doctrine, and the US Navy began building a series of 'super-carriers' to fight what was now clearly a 'Cold War' (i.e. one in which main military forces did not engage). Although not obvious at the time, it is now seen in some quarters as a real conflict, with offensives, strategic withdrawals and mobilisation of technical resources, lasting 50 years. Although there were human casualties they were suffered mostly by surrogate nations and dissident groups, and when victory came, the defeat of the enemy was total.

The Vietnam War followed a superficially similar pattern to the Korean War, but after an interval of little more than a decade, the weaponry deployed by the US forces was altogether different. For the first time aircraft were subjected to surface-to-air missile (SAM) attack and the first 'smart' munitions were used. The US Navy's carriers were heavily engaged, as well as Air Force and Marine Corps aircraft, but yet again, airpower by itself was unable to beat a determined government and its people. When the Americans finally withdrew, the Republic of Vietnam collapsed quickly, just as the critics had warned. It had been an expensive lesson for the United States, which had forgotten an old precept dating from the Second World War: 'never fight on the mainland of Asia'.

The collapse of Soviet Communism in 1989-90, far from initiating a new era of peace, merely complicated matters. Instead of the nuclear balance and the certainties of a bi-polar Cold War world, the military threat to peace was hydra-headed. Former surrogates

HMS Dolphin *was the first permanent base for HM Submarines, occupying Fort Blockhouse at the entrance to Portsmouth Harbour. This post war view shows the prominent escape tower and the enclosed berthing area. With the demise of SSKs in the Royal Navy all SSNs and SSBNs are based at Faslane on the Clyde, leaving* Dolphin *responsible for training.* (SMM)

HMS Thorough *returns to Portsmouth after travelling over 126,000 miles around the world. She left Portsmouth in October 1949 for Sydney, Australia, for training with the Royal Australian and Royal New Zealand navies, before coming home to pay off in December 1957. (CPL)*

were now free to pursue their national aims. The Second Gulf War of 1991 (the first was fought by Iran and Iraq in the 1980s) was precipitated by Iraq's invasion of Kuwait in August 1990. Despite prophecies of disaster, the US-led Coalition defeated Saddam Hussein's 'battle-hardened' armies in two weeks, and with minimal casualties. Although once again the US Air Force claimed to be able to 'bomb Iraq back to the Stone Age', 95 per cent of the stores and munitions went to the Gulf by sea. This did not stop ridiculous claims that the Gulf War was the first won by aircraft unaided, and there was an unedifying attempt after hostilities to denigrate the naval contribution.

One important aspect of the Gulf War was the skilful use of Tomahawk cruise missiles to break through the flanks of Iraq's air defences and to attack the command structure by eliminating targets such as telephone exchanges and power stations. These attacks on land targets were made by surface ships and submarines, giving them a capability to standoff out of the front line yet still project power ashore. On the debit side, however, the Iraqis were able to frustrate an amphibious landing near Kuwait City by laying a huge minefield of influence and contact mines, and inflicted major damage on two US Navy ships.

With the end of the war against Japan in August 1945 the Royal Navy's submarine force was, once more, drastically pruned. All the pre-war boats were sold for scrapping, and a number of wartime boats went because they had seen arduous service. When the procession to the scrapyards was over, the following boats were left:

> 25 'Ts'
> 22 'Ss'
> 16 'As'
> 4 XE midgets
> *Meteorite* ex-German Type XVIIB (experimental)

Design of a new generation of submarines was driven by the need to absorb both the tactical lessons of the war and the technical advances made in Germany. Faulty intelligence about the rate of construction in Soviet shipyards led to a 'submarine scare' in the 1950s, which assumed that hundreds of new fast boats was ready for war. In fact the Soviet Project 613 'Whiskey' was a medium-sized patrol submarine, not an oceangoing type, and many were delivered without engines or combat systems, and were laid up as a material reserve, never to be completed. The first new British design was the *Porpoise*, which proved so successful that it was developed into the *Oberon*. A small number of 'Ts' received a major upgrade to increase underwater speed, but this proved very expensive.

The impact of nuclear power on the submarine cannot be overstated. When the USS *Nautilus* went to sea in 1955 the Royal Navy knew that it had to acquire a nuclear capability if it was to remain a front-line force. The Soviet Navy was also trying to make up lost ground with its own SSN programme. Although the Dounreay reactor was under development progress was very slow, and the decision was taken to acquire a reactor plant for the Royal Navy from the US Navy. This had the desired effect, and by the late 1970s the Navy was running six SSNs.

The success of the US Navy's Polaris missile gave the British Government an affordable alternative to the airborne nuclear deterrent, and the missile and its fire control system was made available for the Royal Navy's own nuclear-powered ballistic missile submarine (SSBN) programme. Like the first SSN, HMS *Dreadnought*, the *Resolution* class SSBNs were delivered on time and within budget, a rare event in British defence procurement. They were run with Port and Starboard crews to maximise the time spent on patrol; the deterrent role demanded that one SSBN should always be on patrol at all times, difficult to achieve with only four boats.

In the 1980s the Cold War showed no sign of abating, and two new classes of SSN were introduced, the 'S' and 'T' designs, as well as the 'U' class of diesel-electric boats

HMS Alderney *(left) and* HMS *Alaric at Gibraltar in the late 1940s, with the depot ship* Forth *and two 'Ts' in the background.* (Author's collection)

(SSKs). The ageing 'R' class SSBNs also had to be replaced, leading to fresh negotiations with the US Navy. As a result the D5 Trident II missile system was leased, and installed in four new 'V' class SSBNs, the last of which joined the fleet at the end of 2000. A design for a new class of SSN, designated *SSN-20*, was stopped, but late in the last decade of the 20th Century design work started on a much more advanced design, the *Astute*.

Much of what Royal Navy SSNs and SSKs achieved during the Cold War has never been made public, but occasionally the curtain is lifted. A US Navy captain recently claimed that the working arrangements between the US Navy and the Royal Navy submarine forces amounted to the greatest 'alliance within an alliance' of all time, with shared expertise, experience and know-how at all levels.

Late 1945 Five surrendered Type XXI U-boats, *U.2529*, *U.3017*, *U.3036*, *U.3041* and *U.3515* taken temporarily into service for trials and evaluation and renumbered *N.27*, *N.41*, *N.28*, *N.29* and *N.30*. In 1946 *N.30* was handed over to the Soviet Union, and *N.27*, *N.28* and *N.29* went the following year. *N.41* was scrapped in 1949, and *U.2518* (not commissioned) was transferred to the French Navy in 1947.

1948 *Taurus* and *Tapir* transferred to Royal Netherlands Navy and renamed *Dolfijn* and *Zeehond*.

11 October 1948 *Saga*, *Spearhead* and *Spur* transferred to Portuguese Navy and renamed *Nautilo*, *Neptuno* and *Narval*.

12 January 1950 *Truculent* (Lt Bowers) sunk in collision with Swedish coaster MV *Divina* off Sheerness. Only eight survivors. The wreck was raised in March and sold for scrap.

The wreck of HMS Truculent *being raised by two giant lifting vessels two months after she was rammed and sunk in the Medway in January 1950. The wreck was scrapped at Grays later that year.* (SMM)

Modernising the 'T' and 'A' classes

Although several of the 'S' class had been modified as targets and for special trials they were too small to warrant major modernisation. HMS *Tradewind* and HMS *Truncheon* were refitted as trial platforms for sensors such as the US Navy's JT hydrophone and the German wartime *Balkon* passive hydrophone and the *Niebelung* active array.

The benchmark for the Royal Navy was the US Navy's highly successful Greater Underwater Propulsion (GUPPY) programme, which provided a new lease of life for wartime patrol submarines by streamlining hulls and doubling battery-capacity. Like the US Navy the Royal Navy recognised that the future for submarines lay in submarine vs submarine warfare, the so-called hunter-killer submarine (SSK) concept.

Between 1951 and 1956 eight welded boats of the *Taciturn* and *Tabard* groups received the 'T Conversion', involving cutting their hulls in two and inserting a 20ft (6-metre) section (14ft only in *Taciturn*). This section contained a second set of motors, clutches to convert all four from direct-drive to diesel-electric, and a fourth battery containing 6560 amp/hour cells. The casing was also streamlined, with fitted retractable or recessed gun and deck fittings, and an enclosed 'fin' replacing the former conning tower. The aim was to achieve an underwater speed of 15kts, but *Totem* logged over 18kts.

The armament was now four bow and two stern 21in tubes. They were intended to launch the new Mk 20(S) 'Bidder' electric passive homing torpedo, but they received the Mk 23 'Grog' wire-guided version. After the withdrawal of the Mk 12 'Fancy' high test hydrogen peroxide (HTP) weapon, the trusty Mk 8 was reintroduced to provide an anti-surface ship capability.

The 'Super Ts' were expensive, and to provide a cheaper alternative, five riveted boats were given the 'T Streamline' modernisation. This involved an enclosed fin, with guns and deck-fittings removed, but no change to propulsion. Although not as capable as the full conversions, they provided useful training for anti-submarine forces, being quieter and faster than before. In October 1952 trials between the streamlined *Tireless* and the unconverted *Tudor* showed an increase of 1.4kts in underwater speed. Higher-capacity 6560 amp/hour batteries replaced the original 5350 amp/hour type. Armament was the same as the 'Super Ts'.

In 1956-60 14 of the 'As' (excluding *Aurochs*) underwent a similar modernisation to the 'Super Ts', with higher-capacity batteries and rebuilt bow and stern, but no change to the propulsion plant. Shortly before being taken out of service *Aeneas* was armed with the Vickers Submarine Launched Air-defence Missile (SLAM), a 'marinised' mounting for Blowpipe missiles on the top of the fin. During the Confrontation between the newly independent Malaysia and Indonesia in 1964 several of the 'As' shipped the venerable 4in gun to deal with blockade-running junks and other small craft. These guns remained long after Confrontation ended.

Between 1964 and 1970 all remaining 'T' class were disposed of, including three sold to Israel. The 'A' class followed in 1970-1977, the last to go being *Andrew*.

HMS Trump *was a fully streamlined 'Super T', with remodelled bow and an enclosed fin. She and her sisters foreshadowed the new* Porpoise *class.* (SMM)

HMS Meteorite, *the salvaged Type XVIIB U-boat, running trials to demonstrate the Walther turbine and its perhydrol (high-test peroxide) fuel. Although never regarded as more than 75 per cent safe,* Meteorite *provided the Royal Navy with enough information to build its own improved version.* (SMM)

The Peroxide Boats

Among the many examples of advanced technology which fell into Allied hands when Germany surrendered, the Walter air-independent propulsion (AIP) system and the Type XXI 'electro' boat were the most intriguing. The Type XXI was in some ways similar to the 'R' class of 1918, combining a streamlined hull with extra-large batteries to achieve a high underwater speed. But it was still a classic diesel-electric submarine, which needed atmospheric oxygen to recharge its batteries. The Walter principle, in contrast, dispensed with atmospheric oxygen by burning an oxygen-enriched HTP fuel to generate steam for a turbine, using a catalyst to release the oxygen.

AIP had long been the Holy Grail of submarine-designers. As early as 1912 the Imperial Russian Navy had run shore tests with a closed-cycle diesel, and between the wars the Kreislauf-cycle engine and the Walter turbine had appeared in Germany. The catastrophic losses inflicted on the U-boats in mid-1943 had forced Admiral Dönitz to turn to his scientists for ways to restore some degree of immunity. The interim solution was the *schnorchel* or 'snort', an air-induction mast which allowed a submarine to recharge her batteries while running at periscope depth. Fitted in pre-war Dutch submarines, it was ignored by both the Royal Navy and the *Kriegsmarine* when they became aware of it in 1940, but in 1943 the Germans were forced to take it seriously, and it became a standard fitting for the U-boats.

In parallel Dönitz put the Type XXI into production and speeded up work on the Walter AIP system. Production difficulties ensured that only three Type XXI boats were operational by May 1945, and work on producing an operational Walter boat was also slower than expected. The Allies found a small number of scuttled Type XVIIBs, and the US Navy and the Royal Navy each recovered one with the intention of evaluating their performance. The navy's *U.1407* was refitted under the supervision of Professor Walter and then commissioned for trials as HMS *Meteorite* in 1948 and ran trials until 1949, when she was sold for scrapping.

Although *Meteorite* was rated as 'only 75 per cent reliable', the trials showed that she could achieve running speeds of 15kts-plus, and her underwater handling was excellent. However, it took 8-10 hours to load only 30 tons of HTP. The fuel, developed from the German Perhydrol, was viscous, and had several unpleasant properties. The slightest impurity in the fuel tank, such as a flake of paint from the deckhead, caused oxygen bubbles to coalesce around it, followed by a rapid rise in temperature and spontaneous combustion. The fire could not be extinguished by foam, as the oxygen fed combustion underneath the foam, and so the porcelain tanks had to be open-topped, allowing them to be drenched with seawater to lower the temperature. A drop of fuel on a sleeve would burn through cloth, flesh and even bone. An even bigger drawback was its cost, some 80 times more than diesel fuel.

Despite these problems the Admiralty embraced the HTP submarine concept eagerly and ordered two boats of an improved design in the 1947 Programme, designated *Ex.14* and *Ex.15*, as well as 12 operational versions for construction in 1949-55. This over-ambitious plan was wrecked by the weakness of the economy and the Korean War, which absorbed scare resources, and the plans were abandoned. When funds were available, the two experimental boats were finally laid down in 1951 as *Explorer* and *Excalibur*, and were launched in 1954 and 1955, entering service in 1956 and 1958 respectively.

HMS Alcide, *a modernised 'A' class, running on the surface in July 1969.* (C & S Taylor)

17 April 1951   *Affray* (Lt Blackburn) failed to surface during Exercise 'Training Spring' in the Channel. Her sister *Ambush* picked up underwater distress signals the following day, but by 19 April the stricken submarine had still not been located. The wreck was finally located in the Hurd Deep on 14 June, 67 miles from St Catherine's Point. The enquiry concluded that the *Affray*'s snort mast had broken off at periscope-depth, and for some reason the induction valve failed to shut automatically as intended. All 72 hands lost, and the wreck still lies 620ft (200 metres) down.

1951   *Tactician*, *Telemachus* and *Thorough* lent to Royal Australian Navy for anti-submarine training, but remained under Royal Navy control.

February 1952   *Satyr*, *Statesman*, *Spiteful* and *Sportsman* transferred to French Navy as anti-submarine training; renamed *Saphir*, *Sultane*, *Siréne* and *Sibylle*.

1952   The Hellenic Navy's *Amfitriti* and *Xifias* were returned to the Royal Navy and reinstated with their original names *Upstart* and *Untiring*. Both sunk as bottom targets in July 1957, off the Isle of Wight and Start Point respectively.

June 1953   *Andrew* crossed Atlantic entirely submerged.

5 March 1954   Launch of *Explorer* at Barrow, first of two experimental high-speed boats running on hydrogen peroxide.

1 October 1954   Launch of *Stickleback* (*X.51*) at Barrow, first of four replacement midgets.

161

The *Explorer* Class

The two vessels of this class, *Explorer* and *Excalibur*, were unarmed and purely experimental. The '*Exploder*' and '*Excruciator*', as they were known because of their periodic mishaps, were very fast for short periods, 25kts-plus, and when completed were the fastest submarines in the world. They were not for the faint-hearted, and their nicknames derived from the frequency with which the entire crew was forced to stand on the casing while dense clouds of white smoke issued from every hatch. They were paid off in 1961 and 1962 respectively, hardly a total success but a considerable technical achievement nonetheless.

Explorer class Specifications

Displacement:	980/1076 tons
Dimensions:	225ft (oa) x 15ft 8in x 18ft 2in
Machinery:	2-shaft Vickers hydrogen peroxide turbine, electric motor, 15,000shp/400shp
Speed:	27kts
Armament:	None
Complement:	41-49

HMS Explorer *(aka 'Exploder'), the first of two experimental high-speed boats driven by an improved Walther turbine using high-test peroxide (HTP) fuel. Speeds attained were phenomenal, but the cost was too much for the limited funds available to the Navy.* (SMM)

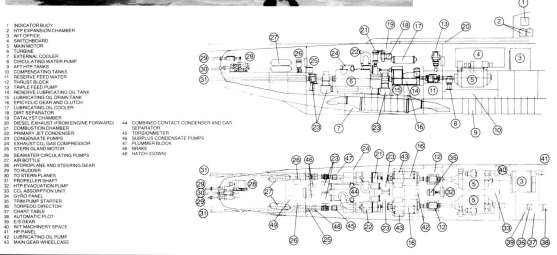

1 INDICATOR BUOY
2 HTP EXPANSION CHAMBER
3 W/T OFFICE
4 SWITCHBOARD
5 MAIN MOTOR
6 TURBINE
7 EXTERNAL COOLER
8 CIRCULATING WATER PUMP
9 AFT HTP TANKS
10 COMPENSATING TANKS
11 RESERVE FEED WATER
12 THRUST BLOCK
13 TRIPLE FEED PUMP
14 RESERVE LUBRICATING OIL TANK
15 LUBRICATING OIL DRAIN TANK
16 EPICYCLIC GEAR AND CLUTCH
17 LUBRICATING OIL COOLER
18 DIRT SEPARATOR
19 CATALYST CHAMBER
20 DIESEL EXHAUST (FROM ENGINE FORWARD)
21 COMBUSTION CHAMBER
22 PRIMARY JET CONDENSER
23 CONDENSATE PUMPS
24 EXHAUST CO_2 GAS COMPRESSOR
25 STERN GLAND MOTOR
26 SEAWATER CIRCULATING PUMPS
27 AIR BOTTLE
28 HYDROPLANE AND STEERING GEAR
29 TO RUDDER
30 TO STERN PLANES
31 PROPELLER SHAFT
32 HTP EVACUATION PUMP
33 CO_2 ABSORPTION UNIT
34 GYRO PANEL
35 TRIM PUMP STARTER
36 TORPEDO DIRECTOR
37 CHART TABLE
38 AUTOMATIC PLOT
39 E/S GEAR
40 W/T MACHINERY SPACE
41 HP PANEL
42 LUBRICATING OIL PUMP
43 MAIN GEAR WHEELCASE
44 COMBINED CONTACT CONDENSER AND GAS SEPARATOR
45 TORSIONMETER
46 SURPLUS CONDENSATE PUMPS
47 PLUMMER BLOCK
48 BRAKE
49 HATCH (DOWN)

Stickleback class midget submarines

These craft may have been initially ordered to replace the old XE craft, but the RN may have intended to use them to 'sneak' a nuclear mine into the approaches to the Soviet naval base at Kronstadt. The project was ultimately unsuccessful, as there were problems finding, and paying for, the necessary fissile material.

Stickleback class Specifications

Displacement:	35.2/39.27 tons
Dimensions:	50ft 8in (pp) 53ft 10in (oa) x 6ft x 7ft 6in
Machinery:	1-shaft diesel-electric, 1 Perkins P6 6cyl diesel, 1 electric motor, 50bhp/44shp
Speed:	6.5/6kts
Armament:	2 detachable 2 ton side-charges
Complement:	5

Stickleback *(ex-X.51) was one of four improved variants of the XE design laid down in 1954-55. They were earmarked for Operation 'Cudgel', a proposal to drop 2-ton nuclear mines in the approaches to Kronstadt in the event of hostilities with the Soviet Union. The payload was equivalent to the Red Beard 2000lb nuclear bomb.* Stickleback *was sold to the Royal Swedish Navy in 1958 and renamed* Spiggen. *(SMM)*

25 February 1955	Launch of *Excalibur* at Barrow, the second *Explorer* class experimental submarine.
16 June 1955	*Sidon* sank at Portland following an explosion of a torpedo being loaded. Admiralty reports ascribed the tragedy to the bursting of a compressed air vessel, but it was in fact a hydrogen peroxide fuelled Mk 12 'Fancy' torpedo, which was soon withdrawn.
25 April 1956	Launch of *Porpoise* at Barrow, first of eight new patrol submarines.
1958	*Sanguine* and *Springer* sold to Israel and renamed *Rahav* and *Tanin*.
18 July 1959	*Oberon* launched at Chatham Dockyard, first of a new class of patrol submarines.

The shattered remains of HMS Sidon *coming to the surface after being sunk on 16 June 1955 by the explosion of a torpedo, while lying alongside a depot ship in Portland Harbour. (SMM)*

HMS Porpoise, *first of a new class of diesel-electric boats built to replace the surviving 'Ts'. With their successors the Oberons, they set the standard for the next 25 years.* (SMM)

The *Porpoise* Class

Apart from the experimental *Explorer* class, the *Porpoise* patrol submarines were the first post war submarines to be ordered, April 1951 and incorporated the wealth of experience available from wartime operations, captured German material and converting the 'T's. With a truly global range of 9000nm (surfaced) the *Porpoise* class proved a success, and were only withdrawn from service after the 1975 Defence Review.

Porpoise class Specifications

Displacement:	1975/2303 tons
Dimensions:	290ft 3in (oa) x 26ft 6in x 18ft 3in
Machinery:	2-shaft Admiralty Standard Range 1 diesels, 2 electric motors, 3680bhp/3000shp
Speed:	12/17kts
Armament:	8-21in TT (6 bow, 2 stern), 30 torpedoes
Complement:	71

HMS Oberon, *first of a new class of diesel-electric boats developed from the* Porpoise *class.* (BAES Marine)

HMS Orpheus *off the west coast of Scotland, against a spectacular backdrop. She and the other* Oberons *were completed with the large dome concealing the Type 187 search sonar.* (SMM)

The *Oberon* Class

The *Oberons* were, when built, the quietest diesel-electric submarines in the world, and highly successful in export markets. In addition to the 13 built for the Royal Navy, six were built for the Royal Australian Navy, three for the Canadian Forces, and four for Brazil. They underwent a major modernisation in the 1980s, with a new bow sonar, Type 2051, a new DCH combat system and the UAL electronic warfare system.

They retained the hullform of the *Porpoise*, and the noise-reduction improvements in the last two, *Sealion* and *Walrus*, but used improved steel to achieve a diving-depth reputed to be 1000ft (300 metres). They saw action in the Falklands in 1982 (minelaying and insertion of Special Boat Service units) and the Gulf War in 1991 (insertion of SBS).

Oberon class Specifications

Displacement:	2030/2410 tons
Dimensions/Machinery/Speed:	as *Porpoise* class
Armament:	originally as *Porpoise* class but modernised to 6-21in TT (bow)
Complement:	64

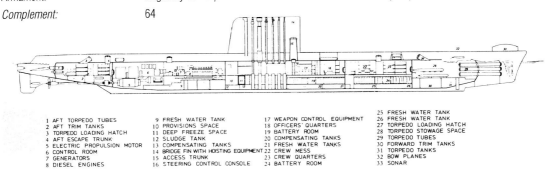

1 AFT TORPEDO TUBES	9 FRESH WATER TANK	17 WEAPON CONTROL EQUIPMENT	25 FRESH WATER TANK
2 AFT TRIM TANKS	10 PROVISIONS SPACE	18 OFFICERS' QUARTERS	26 FRESH WATER TANK
3 TORPEDO LOADING HATCH	11 DEEP FREEZE SPACE	19 BATTERY ROOM	27 TORPEDO LOADING HATCH
4 AFT ESCAPE TRUNK	12 SLUDGE TANK	20 COMPENSATING TANKS	28 TORPEDO STOWAGE SPACE
5 ELECTRIC PROPULSION MOTOR	13 COMPENSATING TANKS	21 FRESH WATER TANKS	29 TORPEDO TUBES
6 CONTROL ROOM	14 BRIDGE FIN WITH HOISTING EQUIPMENT	22 CREW MESS	30 FORWARD TRIM TANKS
7 GENERATORS	15 ACCESS TRUNK	23 CREW QUARTERS	31 TORPEDO TANKS
8 DIESEL ENGINES	16 STEERING CONTROL CONSOLE	24 BATTERY ROOM	32 BOW PLANES
			33 SONAR

21 October 1960   *Dreadnought* launched at Barrow, the RN's first nuclear-powered attack submarine (SSN).

11 May 1961   HMCS *Grilse* (ex-USS *Burrfish*) commissioned at Esquimalt, BC for anti-submarine training. She was the first Canadian submarine since the paying off of *CH.14* and *CH-15* in 1925.

HMS *Dreadnought*

The delays in completing the Dounreay reactor plant for the proposed *Valiant* class forced the Royal Navy to approach the US Navy in 1958, with a view to buying an 'off-the-shelf' Westinghouse S5W plant, the reactor and machinery which drove the contemporary *Skipjack* (SSN-858) class. Although Admiral Rickover showed no willingness in public, it merged later that he was in full agreement, just so long as his approval was kept secret and the Royal Navy accepted his standards of safety and training.

Assembly of the plant was entrusted to Rolls-Royce and English Electric provided the steam turbines, but the overall design of the hull and armament was British. The keel of *Dreadnought* was laid at Barrow on 12 June 1959, she was launched on Trafalgar Day the following year and was completed in April 1963. As a prototype, she completed a long series of deep dives, and as a result she was paid off comparatively early, at Chatham in 1982. The following year she was towed to Rosyth where she remains, along with several other SSNs and SSBNs, awaiting a final decision on disposal of their reactors.

Dreadnought Specifications

Displacement:	3500/4000 tons
Dimensions:	265ft 9in (pp) x 32ft 3in x 26ft
Machinery:	Single-shaft S5W reactor/geared steam turbine, 15,000shp, diesel-electric emergency plant
Speed:	15/28kts
Armament:	6-21in TT, 24 torpedoes
Complement:	88

HMS Dreadnought *was the Royal Navy's first SSN, and added enormously to the Navy's offensive capabilities. (BAES Marine)*

Air Power vs the Submarine

Ever since 1916, when the French *Foucault* was sunk by Austro-Hungarian seaplanes in the Adriatic, the aircraft has been a serious threat to submarines. In 1918 the horrible experience of *C.25* at the hands of German seaplanes pointed the way to developments in the Second World War. The worst danger to the submarine was the high risk of being disabled on the surface by bombs or machine guns, unable to dive.

In the Mediterranean, the North Sea and the Far East submarines were at constant risk from shore-based aircraft, and as late as January 1945 HMS *Shakespeare* received a mauling at the hands of Japanese aircraft. Post-war the capabilities of maritime patrol aircraft were enhanced by radar capable of picking up periscopes and snorts, and in the 1970s the shipborne helicopter emerged as a reliable rapid-reaction anti-submarine aircraft, using dipping sonars and a variety of weapons.

In the absence of fire control, First and Second World War air defence of submarines was largely ineffective. To hit back at the helicopter Vickers designed the Submarine Launched Air-defence Missile (SLAM) system, using 'fire and forget' Blowpipe missiles in a fin-mounted retractable launcher. SLAM underwent trials in HMS *Aeneas* but was not bought - it was asking a lot of submariners to loiter on the surface, deliberately trying to entice a helicopter into range. Since then other systems, notably the Franco-German Polyphem fibre-optically guided missile, have come onto the market, but all such ideas take up valuable internal space, and the Royal Navy's apparent indifference reflects a deep conviction that the safest place for a submarine when hostile aircraft are around is down below. To aid that sort of escape the Navy's SSNs and SSBNs are fitted with electronic support measures (ESM) capable of detecting radar emissions while running at periscope depth.

The RN Goes Nuclear

Although plans to adapt nuclear energy for an AIP system for submarines had been discussed as far back as 1943, a post-war Government directive gave priority to land-based power stations. As a result, serious work on a prototype submarine propulsion system had wait until the mid-1950s. Problems with the Dounreay prototype reactor caused further delays, and in 1958 the US Navy was approached to supply a Westinghouse S5W reactor of the same type as fitted in the *Skipjack* class.

The formidable figure of Admiral Hyman G Rickover USN, 'Father of the Nuclear Submarine' was widely believed to have tried to block the release of such advanced technology to the British, but recently released documents show that Rickover was very much in favour of the deal, but

Diagram showing the arrangement of pressurised water reactor (PWR) nuclear propulsion system as used in Royal Navy nuclear powered submarines.
(Denis Griffiths)

only if his approval was never publicly admitted! The arrangement was in fact two-way, with Royal Navy submarine design expertise made available to the US Navy.

The acquisition of the S5W plant speeded matters up, and HMS *Dreadnought* was basically a British 'front end' and weapons and sensors, with an American 'back end' adapted to British industrial practice and Royal Navy sub-systems. However, according to the former head of nuclear propulsion, Admiral Sir Ted Horlick, cross-fertilisation between the *Dreadnought* project and the Dounreay plant worked to mutual advantage. Although claims have repeatedly been made that all subsequent SSN and SSBN plants are 'American', Horlick and other authorities have stated clearly that subsequent pressurised-water reactors are totally UK-designed, and do not rely on US patents or licences.

HMS *Dreadnought* was also equipped with the Type 2001 'chin' sonar, using Digital Multi-beam Sonar (DIMUS) technology supplied by the US Navy. It was this technology which was targeted by Soviet Intelligence and resulted in the Portland Spy Trial of the 1960s.

Valiant Class

A slightly enlarged version of the *Dreadnought* design was necessary to accommodate the British pressurised water-cooled reactor (PWR). Initially armed with 6-21in bow torpedo tubes, the whole class received the Sub-Harpoon, which *Courageous* deployed operationally in 1981.

Valiant class Specifications

Displacement:	4400/4900 tons
Dimensions:	285ft (pp) x 33ft 3in x 27ft
Machinery:	Single-shaft PWR 1 reactor/geared steam turbine, 15,000shp, diesel-electric emergency plant
Speed:	20/28kts
Armament:	6-21in TT, 26 torpedoes
Complement:	103

HMS Conqueror. (Author's collection)

HMS Resolution *was the first of four strategic submarines (SSBNs) armed with the A3 Polaris submarine-launched ballistic missile (SLBM). They were manned by alternating Port and Starboard crews.* (BAES Marine)

The *Resolution* Class

At the 1962 Nassau Conference the US government agreed to let the Royal Navy buy the Polaris Submarine Launched Ballistic Missile (SLBM) system, to compensate for the cancellation of the Skybolt airborne strategic missile. At a stroke the Royal Navy took over responsibility for the nation's nuclear deterrent from the Royal Air Force.

It was hoped to build five Strategic Nuclear Powered Ballistic Missile Submarines (SSBNs), but the incoming Labour Government cancelled the fifth boat as a sop to its Left Wing. This very short-sighted decision put tremendous pressure on the new SSBN force, as it was pledged to have one submarine on patrol at all times, guarding against a Soviet nuclear strike. But somehow, the SSBNs achieved it, using Port and Starboard crews and a very tight refit schedule.

The design followed the layout of the US Navy's *Lafayette* class, with 16 missile-tubes abaft the fin, in two parallel rows. Propulsion, weapons and electronics were all British. Like the *Dreadnought*, the SSBN programme was brought into service on time and within budget, virtually unknown in modern British defence procurement! The 'bombers' did their job without fuss or incident until the early 1990s, when they were paid off to make way for a new generation.

Resolution class Specifications

Displacement:	7500/8500 tons
Dimensions:	425ft (oa) x 33ft x 30ft
Machinery:	Single-shaft PWR 1 reactor/geared steam turbine, 15,000 shp, diesel-electric emergency plant
Speed:	20/25kts
Armament:	16 Polaris A3 UGM-27C missiles, 6-21in TT
Complement:	143

3 December 1963	*Valiant* launched at Barrow, the first SSN with a British-designed and manufactured nuclear plant.
1964	*Totem* sold to Israel and renamed *Dakar*; sank from unidentified cause en route to Haifa. Wreck located 1999.
9 February 1964	*Ojibwa* launched at Chatham Dockyard, the first of three Canadian *Oberon* type.
1965	*Turpin* sold to Israel and renamed *Leviathan*.
24 September 1965	*Oxley* launched at Greenock, the first Royal Australian Navy submarine since the launch of her namesake in 1926.
15 September 1966	*Resolution* launched at Barrow, the first of a class of four nuclear-powered ballistic missile-armed submarines (SSBNs); armed with the US Navy's A3 Polaris missile.
1968	*Truncheon* sold to Israel and renamed *Dolphin*.

Escape from Sunken Submarines

In the words of a distinguished submariner, anyone who escapes from a sunken submarine has beaten the odds, which are heavily stacked against any escape attempt succeeding. Nevertheless, for reasons of morale, submariners must be given even an outside chance.

The loss of *A.1* forced the Royal Navy to invest in some sort of salvage and rescue organisation. The first escape suit was the Rees-Hall equipment, with a hard helmet and a long-sleeved, belted tunic, but there is no record of it ever being used.

In 1929 the Davis Submarine Escape Apparatus (DSEA) was introduced, and in spite of its failings it remained in service until the 1950s. Its reputation rested on the escape of eight men from the *Poseidon*, including a terrified Chinese laundryman, but it was complex and the oxygen probably killed more submariners than it saved. The complexity of the escape chamber was cruelly demonstrated in the *Thetis* tragedy, and CO_2 poisoning was a constant risk.

The building of the 100ft Submarine Escape Training Tower at HMS *Dolphin* marked a great improvement in escape training. The *Truculent* disaster led to the provision of inflatable immersion suits capable of protecting escapees from hypothermia. After analysis of wartime accidents it was decided that the first priority must be to get people out; nothing complicates a rescue as much as the urgent need to save survivors. Ideally, if everyone alive gets out, salvage can be done at a safer pace, and it is likely that some of the survivors will help the salvage team to understand the cause of the loss.

One-man escape chambers were introduced in the *Porpoise* and *Oberon* classes, and the concept of 'free escape' replaced the oxygen of the DSEA. In effect the escapee rises naturally to the surface, taking care only to breathe out regularly to equalise the pressure in his lungs. But the method only works at relatively shallow depths, whereas nuclear submarines operate at much greater depths. To solve the problem, the Royal Navy collaborates with the US Navy's Deep Submergence Rescue Vessel (DSRV) system. This is a self-propelled midget submarine designed to 'mate' with an escape hatch to form an airlock through which escapees can pass.

The Royal Navy does not own any DSRVs, and merely relies on the US Navy for rapid response (the DSRV is air-transportable). But it is an ageing system, and the Royal Navy is leading a project to create a new NATO rescue system, in which the partners share the development costs.

HMS Andrew, *showing her Mk 23 4in gun on the casing.* (SMM)

2 December 1968   HMCS *Rainbow* (ex-USS *Argonaut*) commissioned at Esqimalt, BC; she replaced the *Grilse* (qv).

1 July 1971   *Artemis* sank at her moorings at HMS *Dolphin* when water entered through the after torpedo hatch. No lives were lost, but she was not repaired.

7 July 1971   *Swiftsure* launched at Barrow, first of a new class of six second-generation SSNs.

HMS Superb *and her five sisters of the* Swiftsure *class were a major improvement over the* Churchill *design, and five are still in service.* (BAES Marine)

The *Swiftsure* and *Trafalgar* Classes

Currently the Royal Navy SSN force comprises five *Swiftsure* class and seven *Trafalgar* class, built between 1969 and 1991. The *Swiftsure* design broke new ground, and marked a break with the previous *Churchill* class in operational capabilities. Originally there were six *Swiftsures*, but the first of class, having carried out a series of deep dives, was bound to have a shorter hull-life than her sisters. She started a refit in October 1988 planned to last 30 months, but cracks in the reactor pressure vessel were discovered, and she was taken out of service in May 1992. Her hull is still awaiting a decision on disposal of the reactor. During her first of class trials she is said to have dived accidentally to 50 per cent more than her crush-depth, surviving the most severe test imaginable. Later she was 'pooped' by a following sea, and the water rushed down the main hatch, disabling the electrical system.

The *Trafalgar* design has a very similar hullform fabricated from NQ-1 steel (similar to the US Navy's HY 80), but internal arrangements are greatly improved. *Trafalgar* was given a conventional 7-bladed skewback propeller, but the rest of the class have pumpjet propulsors, trading off top speed for greatly reduced noise. The diving depth is 300 metres (nearly 1000ft), tested to a maximum of 590 metres (nearly 2000ft). The hull is covered with over 26,000 rubber anechoic tiles to dissipate and absorb sonar pulses.

Both classes are planned to undergo major mid-life upgrades, with the Type 2076 integrated sonar suite, but the main sonar has been delayed. Since late 2000 HMS *Torbay* has been running trials of a new large flank array, assumed to be part of the 2076 system.

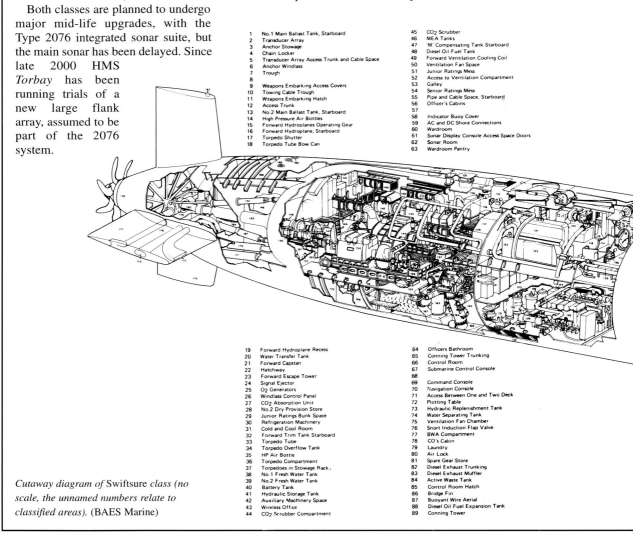

1	No.1 Main Ballast Tank, Starboard
2	Transducer Array
3	Anchor Stowage
4	Chain Locker
5	Transducer Array Access Trunk and Cable Space
6	Anchor Windlass
7	Trough
8	
9	Weapons Embarking Access Covers
10	Towing Cable Trough
11	Weapons Embarking Hatch
12	Access Trunk
13	No.2 Main Ballast Tank, Starboard
14	High Pressure Air Bottles
15	Forward Hydroplanes Operating Gear
16	Forward Hydroplane, Starboard
17	Torpedo Shutter
18	Torpedo Tube Bow Can

45	CO2 Scrubber
46	MEA Tanks
47	'M' Compensating Tank Starboard
48	Diesel Oil Fuel Tank
49	Forward Ventilation Cooling Coil
50	Ventilation Fan Space
51	Junior Ratings Mess
52	Access to Ventilation Compartment
53	Galley
54	Senior Ratings Mess
55	Pipe and Cable Space, Starboard
56	Officer's Cabins
57	
58	Indicator Buoy Cover
59	AC and DC Shore Connections
60	Wardroom
61	Sonar Display Console Access Space Doors
62	Sonar Room
63	Wardroom Pantry

19	Forward Hydroplane Recess
20	Water Transfer Tank
21	Forward Capstan
22	Hatchway
23	Forward Escape Tower
24	Signal Ejector
25	O2 Generators
26	Windlass Control Panel
27	CO2 Absorption Unit
28	No.2 Dry Provision Store
29	Junior Ratings Bunk Space
30	Refrigeration Machinery
31	Cold and Cool Room
32	Forward Trim Tank Starboard
33	Torpedo Tube
34	Torpedo Overflow Tank
35	HP Air Bottle
36	Torpedo Compartment
37	Torpedoes in Stowage Rack
38	No.1 Fresh Water Tank
39	No.2 Fresh Water Tank
40	Battery Tank
41	Hydraulic Storage Tank
42	Auxiliary Machinery Space
43	Wireless Office
44	CO2 Scrubber Compartment

64	Officers Bathroom
65	Conning Tower Trunking
66	Control Room
67	Submarine Control Console
68	
69	Command Console
70	Navigation Console
71	Access Between One and Two Deck
72	Plotting Table
73	Hydraulic Replenishment Tank
74	Water Separating Tank
75	Ventilation Fan Chamber
76	Snort Induction Flap Valve
77	BWA Compartment
78	CO's Cabin
79	Laundry
80	Air Lock
81	Spare Gear Store
82	Diesel Exhaust Trunking
83	Diesel Exhaust Muffler
84	Active Waste Tank
85	Control Room Hatch
86	Bridge Fin
87	Buoyant Wire Aerial
88	Diesel Oil Fuel Expansion Tank
89	Conning Tower

Cutaway diagram of Swiftsure *class (no scale, the unnamed numbers relate to classified areas).* (BAES Marine)

The *Swiftsure* Class

Displacement: 4200/4900 tons
Dimensions: 272ft (pp) x 32ft 4in x 27ft
Machinery: Single-shaft PWR 1 reactor, 2 geared steam turbines, 15,000shp, 4000bhp emergency diesel-electric plant
Speed: 20/30kts
Armament: 5-21in TT (21 Tigerfish Mk 24 Mod 2 torpedoes, 4 Sub Harpoon missiles, later Spearfish torpedoes and BGM-109 Tomahawk)
Complement: 116

The *Trafalgar* Class

Displacement: 4700/5200 tons
Dimensions: 280ft 2in (pp) x 32ft 2ins x 31ft 3ins
Machinery: Single-shaft PWR 1 nuclear reactor, 2 geared steam turbines, 15,000shp, 4000bhp emergency diesel-electric plant
Speed: 20/30kts
Armament: 5-21in TT (21 torpedoes, 4 missiles, with Tomahawk to be added)
Complement: 97

90 Sonar Scanner
91 Navigation Platform
92 Navigation Platform Covers
93 Bridge Fin Shutters
94 Periscope
95 Periscope
96 Shutter Operating Gear
97 Emergency Whip Aerial
98 Radar Mast
99

117 Buoyant Aerial Float
118 Manoeuvring Room
119 Health Physics Lab.
120 De-gaussing Cabinet
121 Electrical, Throttle and Reactor Panels
122 Auxiliary Machinery Panel
123 Reactor Plant Auxiliary Panel
124 RCFW Pump
125 Switchboard Room
126 HP Bilge Pump and Ballast Pump
127 Diesel Generator
128 AC/DC Motor Generator, Starboard
129 Fresh Water/Salt Water Heat Exchanger (Reactor Loop)
130 Make-up System Treatment System
131 HP Make-up Pumps
132 'O' Compensating Tank Starboard
133 Aft Escape Tower
134 SSE
135 Engine Room Hatch
136 Main Steam System Pipework
137 Feed Water Surge Tank Starboard
138 Shore Steam Connection
139 Oxygen Generators
140 Air Treatment Unit
141 Hydraulic Replenishment Tank
142 Emergency Propulsion Motor
143 Port Turbo-Generator
144 Main Turbine Starboard
145 Main Gearbox
146 Shaft Flexible
147 Main Shaft
148 Thrust Block

161 HP Air Compressor
162 Fresh Water Pump
163 Distiller
164 FW/SW Heat Exchanger (Skips Loop)
165 Reserve Feed Tank
166 Bilge Tanks and Reserve Feed Tanks
167 Main Condenser Starboard
168 Lubricating Oil Tanks
169 Lubricating Oil Cooler
170 Brine Tank
171 Condenser Circulating Water Suction Line
172 Condenser Circulating Water Discharge Line
173 Lower Rudder
174 Circulating Water Inlet
175 Circulating Water Outlet
176 Stabilised Fin
177 Starboard Aft Hydroplane
178 Rope Guard
179 Hydroplane Yoke
180 Propeller Shaft
181 Free Flood Space
182 Upper Rudder
183 Aft Anchor Light
184 No.4 Main Ballast Tank, Starboard
185 Shaft Tube
186 No.3 Main Ballast Tank, Port
187 Hydroplanes and Rudders Operating Linkage Guide Tube
188 No.3 Main Ballast Tank, Starboard
189 No.3 MBT Vent Valve, Starboard
190 No.4 MBT Vent Valves
191 Coolant Sampling Cabinet
192
193
194 Emergency Cooling Air Delay Tank
195 Tornel Blower
196 RCFW Valve Chest
197 After Capstan

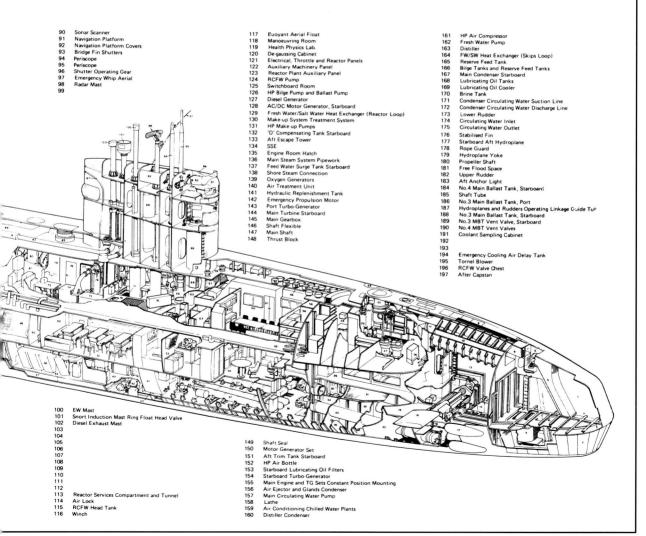

100 EW Mast
101 Snort Induction Mast Ring Float Head Valve
102 Diesel Exhaust Mast
103
104
105
106
107
108
109
110
111
112
113 Reactor Services Compartment and Tunnel
114 Air Lock
115 RCFW Head Tank
116 Winch

149 Shaft Seal
150 Motor Generator Set
151 Aft Trim Tank Starboard
152 HP Air Bottle
153 Starboard Lubricating Oil Filters
154 Starboard Turbo-Generator
155 Main Engine and TG Sets Constant Position Mounting
156 Air Ejector and Glands Condenser
157 Main Circulating Water Pump
158 Lathe
159 Air Conditioning Chilled Water Plants
160 Distiller Condenser

HMS Trafalgar, *first of a new class of seven SSNs. The hullform was developed from the* Swiftsure *design, but internal layout was much improved and NQ-1 steel increased diving-depth to 300 metres. Until the* Astute *enters service in 2005 the* Trafalgars *will form the main strength of the Navy's submarine force.* (SMM)

Other Commonwealth Submarine Operators

The Indian Navy acquired six Project 641 'Foxtrot' type SSKs from the Soviet Union in 1970-74, as part of its long-term plan to become the dominant naval power in the region. To supplement them four IKL Type 1500 SSKs were ordered from Germany at the end of 1981, two to be built at Kiel and two at Bombay (now Mumbai). Although a more advanced design (or possibly because of it), construction of the second pair took much longer than the German-built pair, and was accompanied by considerable acrimony.

Nine Project 877EM 'Kilo' type SSKs were also bought from the Soviet Union in the 1980s, but the biggest shock to India's neighbours was the five-year lease of a Project 670A 'Charlie I' type nuclear-powered boat, an SSGN but minus the cruise missiles. INS *Chakra* conferred great prestige, but her period in service was not satisfactory; she was returned in 1991 and a reported lease of a sister, to be called *Chitra*, was cancelled. The avowed intention was to design and build an SSN in India, but this project has been plagued by delays. In 2000 it was confirmed that a conventionally-powered Project 75 design was under development, which turned out to be the French 'Scorpène' type.

Pakistan had little option but to reply, and in 1964 the Navy acquired the SSK USS *Diabolo* on loan, renaming her PNS *Ghazi*, but she was sunk by Indian surface ships in 1971, during the Indo-Pakistan War. Between 1967 and 1970 three *Daphné* type were built in France, and a fourth unit was bought from Portugal in 1975. Two *Agosta* type ordered by South Africa were embargoed in 1978 were quickly bought by Pakistan, bringing the submarine force up to six SSKs. In 1994 three more advanced *Agosta-90B* type were ordered in France, to replace the ageing *Daphnés*, and known as the *Khalid* class. These are unusual in being designed for the MESMA AIP system, to be installed in No.3 and then retrofitted to the first two.

Despite persistent rumours there appears to be no move to acquire an SSN from China, although Pakistan has claimed that its new SSKs may be armed with nuclear missiles.

Although South Africa was not a member of the Commonwealth when three *Daphné* type were bought from France in the late 1960s, the country rejoined after the end of apartheid. Three IKL Type 209/1400 boats have been ordered from Germany, the *Umkhonto* ('Spear') class.

In 2000 the Malaysian Navy bought the *Zwaardvis* and *Tijgerhaai* about five years after they had been paid off by the Royal Netherlands Navy, making Malaysia the fourth Commonwealth submarine-operator.

1973 7th Submarine Squadron, based at Singapore, disbanded, when the last boat, *Orpheus*, returned to Portsmouth. Three boats and the depot ship *Forth* had been based there for some years.

1974 *Andrew* fired the last round from her 4in deck gun, marking the end of guns in HM Submarines. Her CO signalled to the Admiralty, 'The reek of cordite has passed from the Royal Navy's Submarine Service. Last gun action conducted at 03 1330Z. May the art of submarine gunnery rest in peace but never be forgotten'.

1979 *Alliance* placed on blocks at the Royal Navy Submarine Museum in Gosport. She had paid off six years earlier.

April 1981 *Holland No.1* located off Plymouth, where she sank in 1913 in tow *en route* to the breakers; she was raised and has been preserved on dry land at the Royal Navy Submarine Museum. The wreck of *Holland No.5* has also been located, but she will not be raised.

1 July 1981 *Trafalgar* launched at Barrow, first of a new class of even SSNs, developed from the *Swiftsure* design.

1981 *Courageous* evaluated the US Navy's Sub Harpoon tube-launched anti-ship missile, conducting firings at Point Mugu, California; later that year she became the first SSN in the Royal Navy to have an operational Sub Harpoon capability.

April 1982 *Onyx* 'inserted' SBS special forces teams during the Falklands Campaign, and *Osiris* laid mines.

HMS Alliance *on display at the Royal Navy Submarine Museum in Gosport.* (SMM)

The Sinking of the *General Belgrano*

No other event in the recent history of the Royal Navy has aroused more controversy than the torpedoing of the old ex-US Navy cruiser ARA *General Belgrano* by HMS *Conqueror*. The *Conqueror* was one of a number of SSNs sent to the South Atlantic as soon as the Argentine occupation of South Georgia and the Falkland Islands was confirmed at the start of April 1982.

The SSNs were given a number of specific tasks. One was to tail the aircraft carrier ARA *Veinticinco de Mayo*, another (*Conqueror*) was to tail the surface action group centred on the *General Belgrano*, and a third was to track the whereabouts of a third group, known to be moving on the Falklands in an attempt to trap the Task Force's two carriers in a pincer movement. HMS *Valiant* and two others were hurriedly fitted with an advanced communications intercept (COMINT) system supplied by the US Navy, and stationed on a picket line between southern Argentina and the islands, to monitor air strikes by the Argentine Air Force and the Navy.

Conqueror was using a new sensor, the 2026 clip-on towed array, and thus had no difficulty in picking the propeller-noise of the cruiser and her escorting destroyers. Since the detection-range of 2026 was as much as 200 miles it was easy for the SSN to maintain discreet surveillance without revealing her presence. There was a problem, however, when the Argentine ships approached the Bordwood Bank, an underwater ridge. The long array trailing astern might all too easily be snagged on the ridge. As it was not possible to reel in the array, if it was released or torn away there was a definite possibility that a sudden change of direction by the enemy ships would shake off their pursuer.

The CO, Commander Chris Wreford-Brown, sent a brief message to Fleet HQ in Northwood, asking for updated rules of engagement. On the authority of the Chief of the Defence Staff, Admiral Sir Terence Lewin, permission was given to attack rather than risk a devastating attack on the Task Force. Accordingly, HMS *Conqueror* increased speed to close the gap, and fired three Mk 8 free-running torpedoes. One blew the bow off the *General Belgrano* and the other two hit amidships, fatally damaging her. In the confusion, efforts to co-ordinate damage control were largely unsuccessful, and in the freezing waters of the South Atlantic over 800 men drowned or died of exposure.

An immense amount of speculative nonsense was generated at the time and for a long time after. But Sir Terence Lewin made no apologies for ordering the attack, maintaining that the safety of the Task Force was paramount. His firm stance was successful, for thereafter the Argentine surface forces returned to harbour, and left the prosecution of the campaign to the Air Force and Navy pilots, who paid a heavy price.

The SSN HMS Conqueror *returns to the Gareloch in 1982, flying the Jolly Roger to denote the sinking of the Argentine cruiser* General Belgrano. *This was the first engagement by any nuclear-powered submarine, and the first time a Jolly Roger was flown since 1945. (SMM)*

2 May 1982 *Conqueror* sinks the Argentine cruiser *General Belgrano* with three torpedoes. This engagement also saw the first use of the 2026 towed sonar array for long-range surveillance.

1982 *Dreadnought* paid off at Chatham and towed to Rosyth in 1983, where she remains, awaiting a decision on the disposal of her reactor-core.

2 December 1986 *Upholder* launched at Barrow, first of a new class of diesel-electric boats (SSKs), but destined to be the RN's last.

The *Upholder* Class

The first public mention of a requirement for a new 'conventional' submarine was in 1979, when it announced that the *Oberon* class would be replaced. Their operational role was reconnaissance in waters too shallow for SSNs, and to provide training. A requirement for 12 boats was cut to ten, and then the 1990-91 Defence Review cut the class down to four. By this time the Cold War was over, and it was decided that the reconnaissance mission was no longer needed, and in the harsh financial climate, the Royal Navy could not afford to run two maintenance organisations, one geared to diesel-electric boats, the other to nuclear-powered boats. These fine boats were taken out of service in 1994 and laid up at Barrow in the hope of finding a purchaser. Finally they were leased to the Canadian Forces as the *Victoria* class for five years, with an option to buy later.

Upholder class Specifications

Displacement:	2220/2455 tons
Dimensions:	230ft 7in (oa) x 25ft x 17ft 8in
Machinery:	Single-shaft diesel-electric, 4070bhp, 5400shp electric motor
Speed:	12/20kts
Armament:	6-21in TT, 16 Tigerfish Mk 24 Mod 2 torpedoes, 4 UGM-84C Sub Harpoon missiles
Complement:	47

The Upholder *class diesel-electric boats (SSKs) were intended to replace the* Oberons, *and ten were planned, but only four were built, and in the aftermath of the end of the Cold War they were declared surplus to requirements. They have, however, been leased to Canada as the* Victoria *class.* (BAES Marine)

HMS Turbulent *at the North Pole in 1987 carrying out under-ice trials of the Tigerfish Mk 24 Mod 2 torpedo, with* HMS Superb. *At the same time the US Navy's Mk 48 M 5 ADCAP failed the test.* (SMM)

HMS Opossum *passing the Round Tower in Portsmouth on her return from the Gulf War in 1991, still wearing her 'desert' camouflage. Her mission remains a secret but clearly she landed and recovered special forces for reconnaissance. She has the faired sonar dome, indicating the Type 2051 sonar added during modernisation.* (SMM)

1987 *Superb* and *Turbulent* surface at the North Pole to conduct successful under-ice trials of the Tigerfish Mk 24 Mod 2 torpedo.

January 1991 *Opossum* inserted SBS special forces teams during Operation 'Desert Storm', the Second Gulf War.

Vanguard: A New Generation of SSBNs

In 1980 the UK Ministry of Defence announced that it would build four submarines armed with the C4 Trident UGM-93A SLBM, to replace the ageing *Resolution* class. As it turned out the US Navy withdrew the C4 Trident I from production and switched to the much more capable D5 Trident II, and the Royal Navy had no choice but to follow suit. A deal was struck with the US Department of Defense, whereby the Royal Navy leases the Trident missiles and fire control, and uses US Navy maintenance facilities at King's Bay, GA to support the system, a very big saving.

The *Vanguard* design did not follow the pattern of the US Navy's *Ohio* class SSBNs, and stuck to the 16 tubes of the previous design. They were the first to have the new PWR 2 reactor and the Submarine Command System (SMCS), among other innovations. With the end of the Cold War they changed to a more relaxed routine, with only one crew per boat, but the design allows for longer periods between refits, and it still possible to keep one on patrol at all times. The statistics are very impressive, and the boats are the largest ever built for the Royal Navy. Although the Trident missiles could deliver a total of 96 independently targeted warheads, as a gesture towards nuclear disarmament by 1999 the number had been reduced to 48.

Vanguard class Specifications

Displacement:	14,000/15,900 tons
Dimensions:	491ft 9in (oa) x 42ft x 39ft 3in
Machinery:	Single-shaft PWR 2 nuclear plant, geared steam turbines, 27,000shp, 2700bhp diesel-electric emergency plant
Speed:	20/25kts
Armament:	16 D5 Trident II missiles, 4-21in TT
Complement:	135

HMS Vigilant *is the third of four* Vanguard *class SSBNs built to replace the* Resolution *class. They are armed with the D5 Trident II SLBM, with a range of 6000 miles.* (BAES Marine)

HMS Opportune *making a controlled basin dive in No.5 Basin at Devonport, before starting sea trials.* (Devonport Management Ltd.)

4 March 1992 *Vanguard* launched at Barrow, first of a new class of four SSBN replacements, armed with the D5 Trident II missile.

28 August 1993 HMAS *Collins* launched at Adelaide, the first of six Swedish Type 471 boats ordered to replace the *Oxley* class.

26 May 1994 *Vanguard* fires her first Trident missile off Cape Canaveral, Florida.

October 1995 UK Government signed a Memorandum of Understanding to buy 67 Block III Tomahawk Land Attack Missiles (TLAMs) for installation in Royal Navy submarines. This was to meet Staff Requirement (Sea) 7598, and was to provide sufficient TLAMs to arm two *Swiftsure* class and five *Trafalgar* class SSNs. In July 1998 the Strategic Defence Review announced that all SSNs would eventually receive TLAM, including the future *Astute* class.

1 May 1998 *Splendid* sailed from Rosyth, the first Royal Navy SSN armed with Tomawk cruise missiles.

2 July 1998 Agreement between the Canadian and UK governments and GEC Marine signed for the lease and support of the four *Upholder* class SSKs. At a cost of Can$610 million (£254 million) the agreement provides for a 'lease and buy', giving the Canadians an eight-year lease, with the right to buy them outright at the end of the lease. They are now known as the *Victoria* class.

October 1998 *Trenchant* was visiting Lisbon when a steam leak occurred in the reactor compartment. She was towed back to Devonport for repairs.

18 November 1998 *Splendid* fired a live Tomahawk cruise missile on the Point Mugu test-range in California.

March 1999 *Splendid* launched 20 TLAMs against targets in Serbia.

HMS Trafalgar *being winched into No.14 Dock at Devonport Dockyard for her first of class refit and refuelling.* (Devonport Management Ltd.)

The *Astute* Design

The Royal Navy is buying three *Astute* class SSNs, at a cost of £2 billion including through-life support, to replace the old *Swiftsure* class. The contract includes an option to buy two more and construction on HMS *Ambush*, the second submarine of the class, is due to start later in 2001 with the third, HMS *Artful*, following later. In addition more are likely to be ordered, at least one and possibly as many as seven.

The most notable feature of the design is a jump in size, with displacement twice that of the *Trafalgar* class. This increase is driven by several factors: the need for a larger number of weapons, the demands of silencing, and the simplification of construction and upgrading. A large submarine hull is easier to build and quicker to outfit, driving down costs, and easier upgrading controls through-life cost. Studies are already in hand for the follow-on design, known as the Future Attack Submarine (FASM).

Astute class Specifications

Displacement:	6500/7200 tons
Dimensions:	97m x 10.7m x 10m
Propulsion:	Single-shaft PWR-2 reactor; 2 steam turbines; 2 turbo-alternators, 2 diesel alternators; 2 emergency electric motors; retractable emergency propeller; pumpjet propulsor for main drive
Speed:	29kts
Armament:	6-533mm launch tubes Spearfish Mod 1 torpedoes UGM-109 Tomahawk Block III TLAM missiles UGM-84 Block I anti-ship missiles (stowage for 38 weapons)
Command System:	SMCS
Sensors:	2076 integrated sonar suite (bow, flank and towed arrays) UAP(4) ESM (in first three) I-band navigation radar 2 CM010 non-penetrating periscope masts
Complement:	12 officers, 86 ratings (+12 berths for training)

HMS Astute *is the largest attack submarine to be built for the Royal Navy and the increased hull size means that she will be much easier and cheaper to build and maintain. Astute will also be the most powerful RN submarine ever built, with six weapons tubes and TLAM embarked providing a substantial increase in firepower compared to her predecessors. (BAES Marine)*

Two Upholder *class SSKs being manoeuvred into No.11 Dock at Devonport Dockyard for remedial work to their torpedo-tubes. By working on two submarines at once DML was able to win the competitive bid, using one working group to do both jobs in sequence.* (Devonport Management Ltd.)

Two Upholder *class in No.11 Dock at Devonport, during rectification of torpedo-tube problems.* (Devonport Management Ltd.)

31 July 2000   HMCS *Onondaga* paid off, the last Canadian *Oberon*.

2 December 2000   HMCS *Victoria* (ex-HMS *Unseen*) commissioned at Barrow.

15 December 2000   HMAS *Otama* paid off at HMAS *Stirling*, in Fremantle, Western Australia. She was the last of the *Oxley* class (*Oberon* type) in the Royal Australian Navy.

December 2000   *Vengeance*, the last Trident-armed SSBN, joined the 1st Submarine Squadron at Faslane.

31 January 2001   Keel of *Astute* laid at BAE Systems Marine's Barrow in Furness shipyard, the first of the third generation of SSNs.

HMS Trenchant *proceeding to sea from HMAS* Stirling, *Fleet Base West in Fremantle, WA, in July 1997. In the foreground HMS* Trafalgar *salutes her homeward bound sister.* (RAN)

Appendix 1: Armament of HM Submarines

Torpedoes

Calibre/Mark[1]	Details
18in[2] (450mm) Mk I	made by Whitehead at Weymouth.
18in Mk II	RGF (Royal Gun Factory) variant of Mk I.
18in Mk VII	Submarine model made by RGF from 1908.
18in Mk VIII	'Heater' model[3] of Mk VII for 'Ds' and 'Es'. Sufficient available by April 1914 to arm 'Fs', 'Ss', 'Vs' and 'Ws'.
21in (533mm) Mk I	Made by RGF from 1908.
21in Mk II	Made by Weymouth and Royal Naval Torpedo Factory (RNTF).
21in Mk IV	Made by RNTF.
21in Mk VIII	The standard weapon from 1930s. Made by Weymouth and RNTF and also under licence by Bliss-Leavitt in US. Used in action in 1982 and then withdrawn.
Mk 12 'Fancy'	HTP-fuelled weapon developed to exploit German wartime technology, but withdrawn after the destruction of HMS *Sidon*.
Mk 20(S)	'Bidder' single-speed electric homing weapon made at Weymouth by Vickers (75 in all).
Mk 22	Cable-set variant of Mk 20(S), dropped in favour of Mk 23.
Mk 23	Wire-guided version of Mk 20(S) developed from German Spinne as 'Mackle (S), and entered service in 1971.
Mk 24 Tigerfish	Wire-guided two-speed homer intended for combined anti-surface/anti-submarine use, but Mod 0 entered service well below designed specification. Mod 1 had anti-surface capability, and a 'get well' programme improved reliability in Mod 2. Mod 1 fired in Falklands campaign, but only to sink the burnt-out RFA *Sir Galahad*. Mod 2 (1986) was the first under-ice capable torpedo in service with a NATO navy.
Spearfish	NSR 7525 replacement for Mk 24, started development in 1981. Various improvements incorporated into Mod 1, which became the production variant.
UGM-84	Sub Harpoon encapsulated anti-ship missile; completed trials in *Courageous* in 1981.
BGM-109	Encapsulated Block IIII Tomahawk land attack cruise missile (TLAM); trials in *Splendid*, which also launched first operational strike. Will probably be replaced by Block IV ('Tactical Tomahawk').

[1] Mark numbers changed from roman to arabic post-1945 for the sake of commonality with the US Navy and NATO, and duplications were avoided thereafter.

[2] Actually 17.7in diameter.

[3] By heating the compressed air in the propulsion system, the torpedo's range was increased, but 'cold' weapons were still used in older boats until 1918.

Guns

Apart from the experimental 12pdr fitted in *D.4*, the installation of guns in HM Submarines was not taken seriously before 1914, but the campaign against Turkish shipping in the Sea of Marmora showed that guns were more cost-effective against 'soft' targets. No complete list can be provided as most of the early guns were simply what was available in the nearest dockyard.

20mm Mk VII	Single Oerlikon cannon added on aft platform of CT in most wartime boats to provide minimal air defence.
2pdr (40mm) pompom	*E.29*.
6pdr (57mm)	*E.11* (1915), *H.1* (1916).
12pdr (3in/76.2mm)	On disappearing mounting in *D.4* on completion; *E.21-E.24* (1915).
3in AA	Fitted in many 'Es', 'Js' 'Ks' and 'Ms'.
3in QF	Fitted in 'G' class and 'J' class (all but *J.3* had 4in QF by 1918).
3in QF	Fitted in Second World War 'S' class (some pre-war boats had a disappearing mounting).

4in QF Mk VI	Mounted in *Swordfish* after she was converted to surface patrol craft.
4in QF Mk VII	Mounted in rearmed *J.5-7* and *L.1, L.3, L.6, L.10,* and *L.12.*
4in BL Mk VIII	*E.2, E.11-12 , E.14, E.21* and *E.25* (1915), *Swordfish.*
4in BL Mk XI	*J.1, K.1-4, K.6-16.*
4in QF Mk IV	Fitted in *Oberon* and *Odin* class, and most subsequent classes.
4in QF PXIII	Fitted in *L.3-12.*
4in QF PIX	Fitted in *L.14-17.*
4in Mk XII	Fitted in most 'T' class and some later 'Ss'; first issued 1919.
4in Mk XXII	Fitted in a few later 'T' class and replaced Mk XII post-war.
4in Mk XXIII	Short-barrelled replacement for the Mk XXII, mounted in a few post-war 'Ts' and the 'A' class, starting with *Aeneas* and *Alaric*, and reappeared in some of the modernised 'As' in the Far East in mid-1960s.
4.7in Mk IX CPXVI	Installed in *Regent, Regulus, Rover, Severn* and *Thames.*
4.7in Mk X	One-off gun for trials in *Perseus.*
5.2in QF Mk I	Twin mounting unique to *X.1.*
5.5in QF Mk I	Planned for *K.15-17* but only mounted in *K.17.*
6in howitzer	Fitted in *E.20* for Dardanelles.
12in (305mm) Mk IX	Spares for *Formidable* class battleships, fitted in special mounting (20° elevation, -5° depression, 15° training).

Appendix 2: Preserved submarines of British design or construction

United Kingdom

ROYAL NAVY SUBMARINE MUSEUM
Haslar Jetty Road, Gosport, Hampshire, PO12 2AS, England

April to October: Daily 10.00 - 17.30. *November to March:* Daily l0.00 - 16.30. Closed 24 December to 1 January

Tel: +44 (0)1705 529217, 765130. *Fax:* +44 (0)1705 511349

www.rnsubmus.co.uk.

email - rnsubs@rnsubmus.co.uk

Alliance
Built by: Vickers-Armstrongs Ltd, Barrow-in-Furness
Laid down: 03/13/1945
Launced: 07/28/1945
Commissioned: 03/11/1947

Refitted and modernised in 1958

The Royal Navy training and static display submarine HMS *Alliance* was donated to the Museum in 1978 and placed on display after a two-year restoration and hull strengthening program.

Holland No.1
Built under licence by: Vickers of Barrow-in-Furness
Laid down: 04/02/1901

Launched: 02/10/01
Commissioned: 02/02/1903

The first Royal Navy submarine HMS *Holland 1* was lost on tow to the breaker's yard off Plymouth in 1913. She was found on the seabed in 1981, raised in September 1982, now salvaged and preserved at the Museum (currently under conservation).

HMS X-24
Built by: Marshall, Sons and Co Ltd.
Laid down: 1943

X-24 is the only remaining example of a British X-Craft which saw service during the Second World War. X-Craft were responsible for the crippling of the *Tirpitz* and *Takao* and four Victoria crosses were awarded to their crews for these extraordinary exploits. *X-24* carried out successful missions in the Norwegian Fjords in 1944.

CHATHAM HISTORIC DOCKYARD
Chatham, Kent, ME4 4TE, England

February to March: Wednesday, Saturday and Sunday 10.00 - 16.00. *April to October:* Daily 10.00 - 18.00.
November: Wednesday, Saturday & Sunday 10.00 - 16.00

Tel: (+44) 1634 823800. *Fax:* (+44) 1634 823801

www.worldnavalbase.org.uk

email - info@chdt.org.uk

S17 *Ocelot* (1962 *Oberon* class)

Builders: H.M. Dockyard, Chatham

Laid down: 17/11/1960

Launched: 05/05/1962

Sold 1992 for scrap

The *Oberon* class was unique as the casing was constructed of glass fibre and alloy, the first time a plastic had been used in submarine construction. *Ocelot* was sold for scrap in 1992 but was purchased from the breaker's by the Chatham Dockyard.

WARSHIP PRESERVATION TRUST, HISTORIC WARSHIPS
East Float, Dock Road, Birkenhead, Wirral, Merseyside, L41 1DJ, England

April to August: Daily 10:00 - 18.00.
September to March: Daily 10.00 to 17.00

Tel: (+44) 0151 650 1573. *Fax:* (+44) 0151 650 1473

www.warships.freeserve.co.uk

S21 *Onyx* (1966 *Oberon* class)

Builders: H.M. Dockyard, Chatham

Laid down: 11/16/1964

Launched: 08/18/1966

Decommissioned in 1991

Onyx was the only non-nuclear submarine to take part in the Falklands War. Her primary role was to land Special Forces. She carried 20 men from the SAS and the Special Boat Squadron (SBS) in addition to her full crew and was so crowded that she was nick-named 'The Sardines's Revenge'.

Australia

WESTERN AUSTRALIAN MARITIME MUSEUM
Cliff Street, Fremantle, Western Australia, WA 6160

Friday and Saturday 11.00 - 16.00. Sunday 10.00 - 16.00.
Anzac Day: 13.00 - 17.00
Closed Good Friday, Christmas Day and Boxing Day

Tel: (08) 9430 6756. *Fax:* (08) 9431 8490

http://www.mm.wa.gov.au

S 70 *Ovens* (1967 *Oberon* Class)

Built by: Scotts Shipbuilding & Engineering Co Ltd.

Laid Down: 17/06/66

Launched: 04/12/67

Decommissioned 1/12/95

During her 26 years of service *Ovens* covered more than 420,000nm. In 1986 she had the distinction of being the first conventional submarine in the world to fire a Harpoon anti-ship

missile. In May 1995 she was Gifted to the Museum, and was officially opened to the public in December 1999.

COMMANDER HOLBROOK SUBMARINE MEMORIAL
Holbrook NSW (New South Wales) 2644, Australia

Tel: (02) 6036 2131

S 59 *Otway* (1966 *Oberon* class)

Build: Scotts Shipbuilding & Engineering Co Ltd.

Laid Down: 29/06/65

Launched: 29/11/66

Commissioned: 22/04/68

Holbrook is a tiny rural town of some 1,500 people located 500km south-west of Sydney and the fascination of the locals with submarines dates back to the First World War, when the town was named "Holbrook" after Commander Norman Holbrook, VC. A replica of Holbrook's original *B11* submarine and a statue of Commander Holbrook are located at the town main square. In 1995 the RAN donated a decommissioned *Otway* submarine (fin and superstructure) and the memorial was opened in June 1997.

AUSTRALIAN NATIONAL MARITIME MUSEUM
Street Address: 2 Murray Street, Darling Harbour, Sydney, NSW 2000, Australia
Postal Address: GPO Box 5131, Sydney, NSW 2001, Australia

February to December: Daily 9.30 - 17.00.
January: Daily 9.30 - 18.00. Closed Christmas Day

Tel: (61) (0)2 9298 3777. *Fax:* (61) (0)2 9298 3780

www.anmm.gov.au/

S60 *Onslow* (1968 *Oberon* class)

Built by: Scotts Shipbuilding & Engineering Co Ltd.

Laid Down: 26/05/67

Launched: 03/12/68

Commissioned 12/22/69

Decommissioned: 03/29/99

Onslow arrived to the museum for permanent display just weeks after her decommissioning ceremony in March 1999 with the official opening following in June 1. In service *Onslow* had sailed 358,068nm which is 16 and a half times around the world. *Onslow* is complete and is preserved very close to operational condition.

Apart from the above submarines the remains of the scuttled *J.3*, *J.7* are located at Swan Island and Hampton, in Port Phillip Bay, Victoria.

Brazil

NAVY CULTURAL CENTER
Av. Alfredo Agache, Rio De Janeiro, Brazil
Tuesday to Sunday, 12:00 - 17:00

Closed on January 1st; Carnival; Holy Week on Friday; November 2; December 24, 25, 31.

Tel: (55) 21 216-5325, 216-6025. *Fax:* (55) 21 216-6191

www.mar.mil.br/~sdm/e_riachuel.htm

Riachuelo S22 *Humaita* (*Oberon* class patrol submarine)

Built by: Vickers Barrow, UK

Laid Down: 04/26/1973

Launched: 09/06/1975

Commissioned: 01/27/1977

Decommissioned: 11/12/1997

Riachuelo was named after the naval battle that took place on 11 June 1865, during the Paraguayan War, between the Paraguayan fleet and part of the Brazilian fleet. She was the seventh ship of the Brazilian Navy to receive this name. After decommissioning in 1997 she was presented to the Brazilian navy general documents service and reclassified as a museum submarine.

Canada

CANADIAN WAR MUSEUM
General Motors Court, 330 Sussex Drive, Ottawa, Ontario, K1A 0M8
Tel: (819) 776-8600

Fax: (819) 776-8623

SS 73 HMCS *Onondaga* (1965 *Oberon* class)

Build by: H.M. Dockyard, Chatham

Laid down: 18/06/1964

Launched: 25/09/1965

Commissioned: 22/06/1967

The *Oberons* were commissioned into the Canadian Navy in the 1960s and *Onondaga* was the last Canadian operational submarine of this class. *Onondaga* was the first of the S22 class (super O's) constructed, which included among many modifications, an inboard battery ventilation system. Although not yet on display, there plans are to cut *Onondaga* into three pieces and take her by barge Ottawa where she will be reassembled and placed on display at the war museum.

Appendix 3: Royal Navy Submariners awarded the Victoria Cross

Lt Norman Holbrook RN	*B.11* sinking *Messudieh*, (13 December 1914)
Cdr Edward Boyle RN	*E.14* reaching the Sea of Marmora, (27 April 1915)
Lt Cdr Martin Nasmith RN	*E.11* in Sea of Marmora, (20 May-8 June 1915)
Lt Cdr Geoffrey White RN	*E.14*'s attack on *Goeben* (P), (28 January 1918)
Lt Richard Sandford RN	*C.3*'s destruction of the Zeebrugge Mole viaduct, (22-23 April 1918)
Lt Cdr Malcolm Wanklyn RN	*Upholder*'s sinking of *Conte Rosso*, (24 May 1941)
PO Thomas Gould RN	*Thrasher*, helping to remove two unexploded bombs from casing, (16 February 1942)
Lt Peter Roberts RN	*Thrasher*, helping to remove two unexploded bombs from casing (with PO Gould), (16 February 1942)
Cdr Anthony Miers RN	*Torbay*, entering Corfu Harbour in pursuit of a convoy and attacking two transports and a destroyer, (4 March 1942)
Cdr John Linton RN	*Turbulent*, sinking 100,000 tons of shipping in North Sea/Mediterranean (P), (1941-March 1943)
Lt Donald Cameron RNR	*X.6*, attack on *Tirpitz*, (22 September 1943)
Lt Godfrey Place RN	*X.7*, attack on *Tirpitz*, (22 September 1943)
Lt Ian Fraser RNR	*XE.3*, disabling HIJMS *Takao*, (31 July 1945)
Ldg Seaman J Magennis RN	*XE.3*, disabling HIJMS *Takao*, (31 July 1945)
	P = posthumous

BIBLIOGRAPHY

Bagnasco G, *Submarines of World War II*, (Poole: Arms & Armour, 1977)

Benson J & Warren C E T, *Above Us The Waves*, (London: Harrap, 1953)

Brenchley F & E, *Stoker's Submarine*, (Sydney: HarperCollins, 2001)

Brown D K, *The Eclipse of the Big Gun* (London: Conway Maritime Press, 1992)

Compton-Hall Cdr R (MBE, RN rtd), *The Underwater War, 1939-1945* (Poole: Blandford, 1982)

——, *Submarine Boats - the beginnings of underwater warfare*, (London: Conway Maritime Press, 1983)

——, *Submarine Pioneers*, (Stroud: Sutton, 1999)

Crawford Capt. M L C (DSC, RN Retd.) *HM S/M Upholder*, (Sussex: Profile, 1972)

Dickison A, *Crash Dive - in action with HMS* Safari *1942-43*, (Stroud: Sutton, 1999).

Edmonds M (ed), *100 Years of The Trade: RN Submarines Past, Present & Future*; (papers presented at September 2000 Submarine Conference at Lancaster University)

Friedman N, *Submarine Design and Development* (London: Conway Maritime Press, 1984)

——, *The Postwar Naval Revolution* (London: Conway Maritime Press, 1986)

——, *Navies in the Nuclear Age* (London: Conway Maritime Press, 1993)

Gardiner R (ed), *Conway's All the World's Fighting Ships, 1906-1921*, (London: Conway Maritime Press, 1997)

Gardiner R (ed), *Conway's All the World's Fighting Ships, 1922-1946*, (London: Conway Maritime Press, 2001)

Gardiner R (ed), *Conway's All the World's Fighting Ships, 1947-1995*, (London: Conway Maritime Press, 1995)

Gray E, *British Submarines in the Great War*, (London: Leo Cooper, 2000)

Harrison A N, CB CVO OBE, BR 3043, *The Development of HM Submarines from Holland No.1 to Porpoise*

Hart, S, *Submarine Upholder*, (London: Oldbourne, 1960)

Hezlet Vice Adm. Sir A, *HMS Trenchant at War*, (Barnsley: Leo Cooper, 2001)

Kemp P J, *The 'T' Class Submarine, The Classic British Design*, (Poole: Arms and Armour, 1990)

——, *British Submarines of World War One*, (Poole: Arms & Armour, 1990)

——, *Midget Submarines of the Second World War* (London: Chatham, 1999)

——, *Submarine Action*, (Stroud: Sutton, 2000)

Le Fleming H M, *Warships of World War I*, (London: Ian Allan, 1961)

Lenton H T & Colledge J J, *Warships of World War II*, (London: Ian Allan, 1962)

Mitchell P, *Chariots of the Sea*, (Huddersfield: Netherwood, 1998)

Parsons W B, *Robert Fulton and the Submarine*, (New York: Columbia University Press, 1922)

Poolman K, *The British Sailor*, (Poole: Arms & Armour, 1989)

Preston A, *Submarines: The history and evolution of underwater fighting vessels*, (London: Octopus Books, 1975)

Roberts D, *HMS Thetis - Secrets and Scandal*, (Merseyside: Avid, 2000)

Robertson T, *The Ship with Two Captains*, (London: Evans, 1957)

Tall Cdr J J and Kemp P, *HM Submarines in Camera*, (Stroud: Sutton, 1996)

Treadwell T C, *Strike from beneath the sea,* (Stroud: Tempus, 1999)

van der Vat D, *Stealth at Sea*, (London: Weidenfeld & Nicholson, 1994)

Warren C & Benson J, *Thetis - The Admiralty Regrets*, (London: Harrap, 1958)

Warship annual; ed by various

Wilson M, *Baltic assignment: British Submariners in Russia 1914-1919*, (London: Leo Cooper, 1985)

Wilson M & Kemp P, *Mediterranean Submarines*, (Wilmslow: Crécy, 1997)

Winton J (ed), *Freedom's Battle: The War at Sea*, 3 volumes (London: Hutchinson, 1970)

Young Cdr. E, DSO, DSC, RNV(S)R, *One Of Our Submarines*, (Ware: Wordsworth, 1997)

INDEX